Mometrix
TEST PREPARATION

Regents

Success Strategies United States History and Government

Dear Future Exam Success Story

First of all, **THANK YOU** for purchasing Mometrix study materials!

Second, congratulations! You are one of the few determined test-takers who are committed to doing whatever it takes to excel on your exam. **You have come to the right place.** We developed these study materials with one goal in mind: to deliver you the information you need in a format that's concise and easy to use.

In addition to optimizing your guide for the content of the test, we've outlined our recommended steps for breaking down the preparation process into small, attainable goals so you can make sure you stay on track.

We've also analyzed the entire test-taking process, identifying the most common pitfalls and showing how you can overcome them and be ready for any curveball the test throws you.

Standardized testing is one of the biggest obstacles on your road to success, which only increases the importance of doing well in the high-pressure, high-stakes environment of test day. Your results on this test could have a significant impact on your future, and this guide provides the information and practical advice to help you achieve your full potential on test day.

Your success is our success

We would love to hear from you! If you would like to share the story of your exam success or if you have any questions or comments in regard to our products, please contact us at **800-673-8175** or **support@mometrix.com**.

Thanks again for your business and we wish you continued success!

Sincerely,
The Mometrix Test Preparation Team

Printed in the United States of America

TABLE OF CONTENTS

Introduction

Thank you for purchasing this resource! You have made the choice to prepare yourself for a test that could have a huge impact on your future, and this guide is designed to help you be fully ready for test day. Obviously, it's important to have a solid understanding of the test material, but you also need to be prepared for the unique environment and stressors of the test, so that you can perform to the best of your abilities.

For this purpose, the first section that appears in this guide is the **Success Strategies**. We've devoted countless hours to meticulously researching what works and what doesn't, and we've boiled down our findings to the five most impactful steps you can take to improve your performance on the test. We start at the beginning with study planning and move through the preparation process, all the way to the testing strategies that will help you get the most out of what you know when you're finally sitting in front of the test.

We recommend that you start preparing for your test as far in advance as possible. However, if you've bought this guide as a last-minute study resource and only have a few days before your test, we recommend that you skip over the first two Success Strategies since they address a long-term study plan.

If you struggle with **test anxiety**, we strongly encourage you to check out our recommendations for how you can overcome it. Test anxiety is a formidable foe, but it can be beaten, and we want to make sure you have the tools you need to defeat it.

Strategy #1 – Plan Big, Study Small

There's a lot riding on your performance. If you want to ace this test, you're going to need to keep your skills sharp and the material fresh in your mind. You need a plan that lets you review everything you need to know while still fitting in your schedule. We'll break this strategy down into three categories.

Information Organization

Start with the information you already have: the official test outline. From this, you can make a complete list of all the concepts you need to cover before the test. Organize these concepts into groups that can be studied together, and create a list of any related vocabulary you need to learn so you can brush up on any difficult terms. You'll want to keep this vocabulary list handy once you actually start studying since you may need to add to it along the way.

Time Management

Once you have your set of study concepts, decide how to spread them out over the time you have left before the test. Break your study plan into small, clear goals so you have a manageable task for each day and know exactly what you're doing. Then just focus on one small step at a time. When you manage your time this way, you don't need to spend hours at a time studying. Studying a small block of content for a short period each day helps you retain information better and avoid stressing over how much you have left to do. You can relax knowing that you have a plan to cover everything in time. In order for this strategy to be effective though, you have to start studying early and stick to your schedule. Avoid the exhaustion and futility that comes from last-minute cramming!

Study Environment

The environment you study in has a big impact on your learning. Studying in a coffee shop, while probably more enjoyable, is not likely to be as fruitful as studying in a quiet room. It's important to keep distractions to a minimum. You're only planning to study for a short block of time, so make the most of it. Don't pause to check your phone or get up to find a snack. It's also important to **avoid multitasking**. Research has consistently shown that multitasking will make your studying dramatically less effective. Your study area should also be comfortable and well-lit so you don't have the distraction of straining your eyes or sitting on an uncomfortable chair.

The time of day you study is also important. You want to be rested and alert. Don't wait until just before bedtime. Study when you'll be most likely to comprehend and remember. Even better, if you know what time of day your test will be, set that time aside for study. That way your brain will be used to working on that subject at that specific time and you'll have a better chance of recalling information.

Finally, it can be helpful to team up with others who are studying for the same test. Your actual studying should be done in as isolated an environment as possible, but the work of organizing the information and setting up the study plan can be divided up. In between study sessions, you can discuss with your teammates the concepts that you're all studying and quiz each other on the details. Just be sure that your teammates are as serious about the test as you are. If you find that your study time is being replaced with social time, you might need to find a new team.

Strategy #2 – Make Your Studying Count

You're devoting a lot of time and effort to preparing for this test, so you want to be absolutely certain it will pay off. This means doing more than just reading the content and hoping you can remember it on test day. It's important to make every minute of study count. There are two main areas you can focus on to make your studying count.

Retention

It doesn't matter how much time you study if you can't remember the material. You need to make sure you are retaining the concepts. To check your retention of the information you're learning, try recalling it at later times with minimal prompting. Try carrying around flashcards and glance at one or two from time to time or ask a friend who's also studying for the test to quiz you.

To enhance your retention, look for ways to put the information into practice so that you can apply it rather than simply recalling it. If you're using the information in practical ways, it will be much easier to remember. Similarly, it helps to solidify a concept in your mind if you're not only reading it to yourself but also explaining it to someone else. Ask a friend to let you teach them about a concept you're a little shaky on (or speak aloud to an imaginary audience if necessary). As you try to summarize, define, give examples, and answer your friend's questions, you'll understand the concepts better and they will stay with you longer. Finally, step back for a big picture view and ask yourself how each piece of information fits with the whole subject. When you link the different concepts together and see them working together as a whole, it's easier to remember the individual components.

Finally, practice showing your work on any multi-step problems, even if you're just studying. Writing out each step you take to solve a problem will help solidify the process in your mind, and you'll be more likely to remember it during the test.

Modality

Modality simply refers to the means or method by which you study. Choosing a study modality that fits your own individual learning style is crucial. No two people learn best in exactly the same way, so it's important to know your strengths and use them to your advantage.

For example, if you learn best by visualization, focus on visualizing a concept in your mind and draw an image or a diagram. Try color-coding your notes, illustrating them, or creating symbols that will trigger your mind to recall a learned concept. If you learn best by hearing or discussing information, find a study partner who learns the same way or read aloud to yourself. Think about how to put the information in your own words. Imagine that you are giving a lecture on the topic and record yourself so you can listen to it later.

For any learning style, flashcards can be helpful. Organize the information so you can take advantage of spare moments to review. Underline key words or phrases. Use different colors for different categories. Mnemonic devices (such as creating a short list in which every item starts with the same letter) can also help with retention. Find what works best for you and use it to store the information in your mind most effectively and easily.

Strategy #3 – Practice the Right Way

Your success on test day depends not only on how many hours you put into preparing, but also on whether you prepared the right way. It's good to check along the way to see if your studying is paying off. One of the most effective ways to do this is by taking practice tests to evaluate your progress. Practice tests are useful because they show exactly where you need to improve. Every time you take a practice test, pay special attention to these three groups of questions:

- The questions you got wrong
- The questions you had to guess on, even if you guessed right
- The questions you found difficult or slow to work through

This will show you exactly what your weak areas are, and where you need to devote more study time. Ask yourself why each of these questions gave you trouble. Was it because you didn't understand the material? Was it because you didn't remember the vocabulary? Do you need more repetitions on this type of question to build speed and confidence? Dig into those questions and figure out how you can strengthen your weak areas as you go back to review the material.

Additionally, many practice tests have a section explaining the answer choices. It can be tempting to read the explanation and think that you now have a good understanding of the concept. However, an explanation likely only covers part of the question's broader context. Even if the explanation makes perfect sense, **go back and investigate** every concept related to the question until you're positive you have a thorough understanding.

As you go along, keep in mind that the practice test is just that: practice. Memorizing these questions and answers will not be very helpful on the actual test because it is unlikely to have any of the same exact questions. If you only know the right answers to the sample questions, you won't be prepared for the real thing. **Study the concepts** until you understand them fully, and then you'll be able to answer any question that shows up on the test.

It's important to wait on the practice tests until you're ready. If you take a test on your first day of study, you may be overwhelmed by the amount of material covered and how much you need to learn. Work up to it gradually.

On test day, you'll need to be prepared for answering questions, managing your time, and using the test-taking strategies you've learned. It's a lot to balance, like a mental marathon that will have a big impact on your future. Like training for a marathon, you'll need to start slowly and work your way up. When test day arrives, you'll be ready.

Start with the strategies you've read in the first two Success Strategies—plan your course and study in the way that works best for you. If you have time, consider using multiple study resources to get different approaches to the same concepts. It can be helpful to see difficult concepts from more than one angle. Then find a good source for practice tests. Many times, the test website will suggest potential study resources or provide sample tests.

Practice Test Strategy

If you're able to find at least three practice tests, we recommend this strategy:

Untimed and Open-Book Practice

Take the first test with no time constraints and with your notes and study guide handy. Take your time and focus on applying the strategies you've learned.

Timed and Open-Book Practice

Take the second practice test open-book as well, but set a timer and practice pacing yourself to finish in time.

Timed and Closed-Book Practice

Take any other practice tests as if it were test day. Set a timer and put away your study materials. Sit at a table or desk in a quiet room, imagine yourself at the testing center, and answer questions as quickly and accurately as possible.

Keep repeating timed and closed-book tests on a regular basis until you run out of practice tests or it's time for the actual test. Your mind will be ready for the schedule and stress of test day, and you'll be able to focus on recalling the material you've learned.

Strategy #4 – Pace Yourself

Once you're fully prepared for the material on the test, your biggest challenge on test day will be managing your time. Just knowing that the clock is ticking can make you panic even if you have plenty of time left. Work on pacing yourself so you can build confidence against the time constraints of the exam. Pacing is a difficult skill to master, especially in a high-pressure environment, so **practice is vital**.

Set time expectations for your pace based on how much time is available. For example, if a section has 60 questions and the time limit is 30 minutes, you know you have to average 30 seconds or less per question in order to answer them all. Although 30 seconds is the hard limit, set 25 seconds per question as your goal, so you reserve extra time to spend on harder questions. When you budget extra time for the harder questions, you no longer have any reason to stress when those questions take longer to answer.

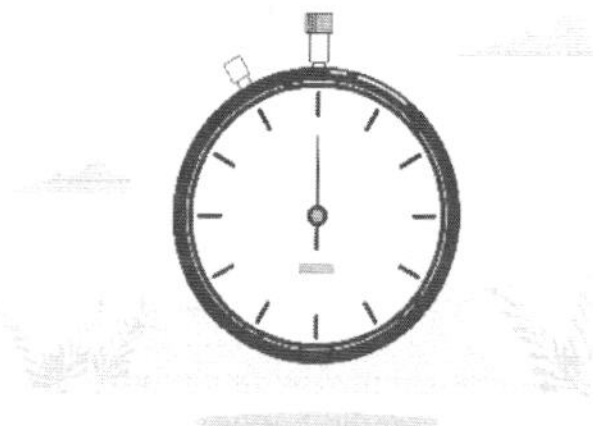

Don't let this time expectation distract you from working through the test at a calm, steady pace, but keep it in mind so you don't spend too much time on any one question. Recognize that taking extra time on one question you don't understand may keep you from answering two that you do understand later in the test. If your time limit for a question is up and you're still not sure of the answer, mark it and move on, and come back to it later if the time and the test format allow. If the testing format doesn't allow you to return to earlier questions, just make an educated guess; then put it out of your mind and move on.

On the easier questions, be careful not to rush. It may seem wise to hurry through them so you have more time for the challenging ones, but it's not worth missing one if you know the concept and just didn't take the time to read the question fully. Work efficiently but make sure you understand the question and have looked at all of the answer choices, since more than one may seem right at first.

Even if you're paying attention to the time, you may find yourself a little behind at some point. You should speed up to get back on track, but do so wisely. Don't panic; just take a few seconds less on each question until you're caught up. Don't guess without thinking, but do look through the answer choices and eliminate any you know are wrong. If you can get down to two choices, it is often worthwhile to guess from those. Once you've chosen an answer, move on and don't dwell on any that you skipped or had to hurry through. If a question was taking too long, chances are it was one of the harder ones, so you weren't as likely to get it right anyway.

On the other hand, if you find yourself getting ahead of schedule, it may be beneficial to slow down a little. The more quickly you work, the more likely you are to make a careless mistake that will affect your score. You've budgeted time for each question, so don't be afraid to spend that time. Practice an efficient but careful pace to get the most out of the time you have.

Test-Taking Strategies

This section contains a list of test-taking strategies that you may find helpful as you work through the test. By taking what you know and applying logical thought, you can maximize your chances of answering any question correctly!

It is very important to realize that every question is different and every person is different: no single strategy will work on every question, and no single strategy will work for every person. That's why we've included all of them here, so you can try them out and determine which ones work best for different types of questions and which ones work best for you.

Question Strategies

☑ Read Carefully

Read the question and the answer choices carefully. Don't miss the question because you misread the terms. You have plenty of time to read each question thoroughly and make sure you understand what is being asked. Yet a happy medium must be attained, so don't waste too much time. You must read carefully and efficiently.

☑ Contextual Clues

Look for contextual clues. If the question includes a word you are not familiar with, look at the immediate context for some indication of what the word might mean. Contextual clues can often give you all the information you need to decipher the meaning of an unfamiliar word. Even if you can't determine the meaning, you may be able to narrow down the possibilities enough to make a solid guess at the answer to the question.

☑ Prefixes

If you're having trouble with a word in the question or answer choices, try dissecting it. Take advantage of every clue that the word might include. Prefixes can be a huge help. Usually, they allow you to determine a basic meaning. *Pre-* means before, *post-* means after, *pro-* is positive, *de-* is negative. From prefixes, you can get an idea of the general meaning of the word and try to put it into context.

☑ Hedge Words

Watch out for critical hedge words, such as *likely, may, can, often, almost, mostly, usually, generally, rarely,* and *sometimes.* Question writers insert these hedge phrases to cover every possibility. Often an answer choice will be wrong simply because it leaves no room for exception. Be on guard for answer choices that have definitive words such as *exactly* and *always.*

☑ Switchback Words

Stay alert for *switchbacks.* These are the words and phrases frequently used to alert you to shifts in thought. The most common switchback words are *but, although,* and *however.* Others include *nevertheless, on the other hand, even though, while, in spite of, despite,* and *regardless of.* Switchback words are important to catch because they can change the direction of the question or an answer choice.

⊘ FACE VALUE

When in doubt, use common sense. Accept the situation in the problem at face value. Don't read too much into it. These problems will not require you to make wild assumptions. If you have to go beyond creativity and warp time or space in order to have an answer choice fit the question, then you should move on and consider the other answer choices. These are normal problems rooted in reality. The applicable relationship or explanation may not be readily apparent, but it is there for you to figure out. Use your common sense to interpret anything that isn't clear.

Answer Choice Strategies

⊘ ANSWER SELECTION

The most thorough way to pick an answer choice is to identify and eliminate wrong answers until only one is left, then confirm it is the correct answer. Sometimes an answer choice may immediately seem right, but be careful. The test writers will usually put more than one reasonable answer choice on each question, so take a second to read all of them and make sure that the other choices are not equally obvious. As long as you have time left, it is better to read every answer choice than to pick the first one that looks right without checking the others.

⊘ ANSWER CHOICE FAMILIES

An answer choice family consists of two (in rare cases, three) answer choices that are very similar in construction and cannot all be true at the same time. If you see two answer choices that are direct opposites or parallels, one of them is usually the correct answer. For instance, if one answer choice says that quantity *x* increases and another either says that quantity *x* decreases (opposite) or says that quantity *y* increases (parallel), then those answer choices would fall into the same family. An answer choice that doesn't match the construction of the answer choice family is more likely to be incorrect. Most questions will not have answer choice families, but when they do appear, you should be prepared to recognize them.

⊘ ELIMINATE ANSWERS

Eliminate answer choices as soon as you realize they are wrong, but make sure you consider all possibilities. If you are eliminating answer choices and realize that the last one you are left with is also wrong, don't panic. Start over and consider each choice again. There may be something you missed the first time that you will realize on the second pass.

⊘ AVOID FACT TRAPS

Don't be distracted by an answer choice that is factually true but doesn't answer the question. You are looking for the choice that answers the question. Stay focused on what the question is asking for so you don't accidentally pick an answer that is true but incorrect. Always go back to the question and make sure the answer choice you've selected actually answers the question and is not merely a true statement.

⊘ EXTREME STATEMENTS

In general, you should avoid answers that put forth extreme actions as standard practice or proclaim controversial ideas as established fact. An answer choice that states the "process should be used in certain situations, if..." is much more likely to be correct than one that states the "process should be discontinued completely." The first is a calm rational statement and doesn't even make a definitive, uncompromising stance, using a hedge word *if* to provide wiggle room, whereas the second choice is far more extreme.

⊘ Benchmark

As you read through the answer choices and you come across one that seems to answer the question well, mentally select that answer choice. This is not your final answer, but it's the one that will help you evaluate the other answer choices. The one that you selected is your benchmark or standard for judging each of the other answer choices. Every other answer choice must be compared to your benchmark. That choice is correct until proven otherwise by another answer choice beating it. If you find a better answer, then that one becomes your new benchmark. Once you've decided that no other choice answers the question as well as your benchmark, you have your final answer.

⊘ Predict the Answer

Before you even start looking at the answer choices, it is often best to try to predict the answer. When you come up with the answer on your own, it is easier to avoid distractions and traps because you will know exactly what to look for. The right answer choice is unlikely to be word-for-word what you came up with, but it should be a close match. Even if you are confident that you have the right answer, you should still take the time to read each option before moving on.

General Strategies

⊘ Tough Questions

If you are stumped on a problem or it appears too hard or too difficult, don't waste time. Move on! Remember though, if you can quickly check for obviously incorrect answer choices, your chances of guessing correctly are greatly improved. Before you completely give up, at least try to knock out a couple of possible answers. Eliminate what you can and then guess at the remaining answer choices before moving on.

⊘ Check Your Work

Since you will probably not know every term listed and the answer to every question, it is important that you get credit for the ones that you do know. Don't miss any questions through careless mistakes. If at all possible, try to take a second to look back over your answer selection and make sure you've selected the correct answer choice and haven't made a costly careless mistake (such as marking an answer choice that you didn't mean to mark). This quick double check should more than pay for itself in caught mistakes for the time it costs.

⊘ Pace Yourself

It's easy to be overwhelmed when you're looking at a page full of questions; your mind is confused and full of random thoughts, and the clock is ticking down faster than you would like. Calm down and maintain the pace that you have set for yourself. Especially as you get down to the last few minutes of the test, don't let the small numbers on the clock make you panic. As long as you are on track by monitoring your pace, you are guaranteed to have time for each question.

⊘ Don't Rush

It is very easy to make errors when you are in a hurry. Maintaining a fast pace in answering questions is pointless if it makes you miss questions that you would have gotten right otherwise. Test writers like to include distracting information and wrong answers that seem right. Taking a little extra time to avoid careless mistakes can make all the difference in your test score. Find a pace that allows you to be confident in the answers that you select.

✓ Keep Moving

Panicking will not help you pass the test, so do your best to stay calm and keep moving. Taking deep breaths and going through the answer elimination steps you practiced can help to break through a stress barrier and keep your pace.

Final Notes

The combination of a solid foundation of content knowledge and the confidence that comes from practicing your plan for applying that knowledge is the key to maximizing your performance on test day. As your foundation of content knowledge is built up and strengthened, you'll find that the strategies included in this chapter become more and more effective in helping you quickly sift through the distractions and traps of the test to isolate the correct answer.

Now that you're preparing to move forward into the test content chapters of this book, be sure to keep your goal in mind. As you read, think about how you will be able to apply this information on the test. If you've already seen sample questions for the test and you have an idea of the question format and style, try to come up with questions of your own that you can answer based on what you're reading. This will give you valuable practice applying your knowledge in the same ways you can expect to on test day.

Good luck and good studying!

United States History

American History Pre-Columbian to 1789

Prior to European colonization, the land that would become the United States was populated by millions of Native Americans belonging to hundreds of distinct tribes. Native American societies were diverse and sophisticated, with political structures, religious beliefs, domesticated animals, agricultural practices, and trade networks. Native Americans adapted their societies and cultures to the environments in which they settled, which led to distinct cultures, beliefs, practices, and languages all across the continent.

Well-Known Native Americans

The following are five well-known Native Americans and their roles in early US history:

1. **Squanto**, an Algonquian, helped early English settlers survive the hard winter by teaching them the native methods of planting corn, squash, and pumpkins.
2. **Pocahontas**, also Algonquian, became famous as a liaison with John Smith's Jamestown colony in 1607.
3. **Sacagawea**, a Shoshone, served a vital role in the Lewis and Clark expedition when the two explorers hired her as their guide in 1805.
4. **Crazy Horse** and **Sitting Bull** led Sioux and Cheyenne troops in the Battle of the Little Bighorn in 1876, soundly defeating George Armstrong Custer.
5. **Chief Joseph**, a leader of the Nez Perce who supported peaceful interaction with white settlers, attempted to relocate his tribe to Canada rather than move them to a reservation.

Major Regional Native American Groups

The major regional Native American groups and the major traits of each are as follows:

- The **Algonquians** in the eastern part of the United States lived in wigwams. The northern tribes subsisted on hunting and gathering, while those who were farther south grew crops such as corn.
- The **Iroquois**, also an east coast tribe, spoke a different language from the Algonquians and lived in rectangular longhouses.
- The **Plains tribes** lived between the Mississippi River and the Rocky Mountains. These nomadic tribes lived in teepees and followed the buffalo herds. Plains tribes included the Sioux, Cheyenne, Comanche, and Blackfoot.
- **Pueblo tribes** included the Zuni, Hopi, and Acoma. They lived in the Southwest deserts in homes made of stone or adobe. They domesticated animals and cultivated corn and beans.
- On the Pacific coast, tribes such as the **Tlingit**, **Chinook**, and **Salish** lived on fish,deer, native berries, and roots. Their rectangular homes housed large family groups, and they used totem poles.
- In the far north, the **Aleuts** and **Inuit** lived in skin tents or igloos. Talented fishermen, they built kayaks and umiaks and also hunted caribou, seals, whales, and walrus.

Review Video: Major Regional Native American Groups
Visit mometrix.com/academy and enter code: 550136

Age of Exploration

The Age of Exploration is also called the **Age of Discovery**. It is generally considered to have begun in the early 15th century and continued into the 17th century. Major developments of the **Age of Exploration** included technological advances in navigation, mapmaking, and shipbuilding. These advances led to expanded European exploration of the rest of the world. Explorers set out from several European countries, including Portugal, Spain, France, and England, seeking new routes to Asia. These efforts led to the discovery of new lands, as well as colonization in India, Asia, Africa, and North America.

Review Video: Age of Exploration
Visit mometrix.com/academy and enter code: 612972

Impact of Technological Advances in Navigation and Seafaring Exploration

For long ocean journeys, it was important for sailors to be able to find their way home even when their vessels sailed far out to sea. A variety of navigational tools enabled them to launch ambitious journeys over long distances. The **compass** and **astrolabe** were particularly important advancements. Chinese navigators used the magnetic compass in approximately 200 BC, and knowledge of the astrolabe came to Europe from Arab navigators and traders who had refined designs developed by the ancient Greeks. The Portuguese developed a ship called a **caravel** in the 1400s that incorporated navigational advancements with the ability to make long sea journeys. Equipped with this advanced vessel, the Portuguese achieved a major goal of the Age of Exploration by discovering a **sea route** from Europe to Asia in 1498.

Significance of Christopher Columbus's Voyage

In 1492, Columbus, a Genoan explorer, obtained financial backing from King Ferdinand and Queen Isabella of Spain to seek a sea route to Asia. He sought a trade route with the Asian Indies to the west. With three ships, the *Niña*, the *Pinta*, and the *Santa Maria*, he eventually landed in the **West Indies**. While Columbus failed in his effort to discover a western route to Asia, he is credited with the discovery of the **Americas**.

Review Video: Christopher Columbus
Visit mometrix.com/academy and enter code: 496598

French, Spanish, Dutch, and British Goals in Colonization of the Americas

France, Spain, the Netherlands, and England each had specific goals in the colonization of the Americas:

- Initial **French colonies** were focused on expanding the fur trade. Later, French colonization led to the growth of plantations in Louisiana, which brought numerous African slaves to the New World.
- **Spanish colonists** came to look for wealth and to convert the natives to Christianity. For some, the desire for gold led to mining in the New World, while others established large ranches.

- The **Dutch** were also involved in the fur trade and imported slaves as the need for laborers increased.
- **British colonists** arrived with various goals. Some were simply looking for additional income, while others were fleeing Britain to escape religious persecution.

> **Review Video: European Colonization of the Americas**
> Visit mometrix.com/academy and enter code: 438412

Interactions Between the Colonies and Native Americans

While there were examples of peaceful relations between Native Americans and European colonists, these two groups were often in conflict. The colonists constantly attempted to expand their territories and take Native American land. Native Americans often tried to stop the expansion of European colonies via war and diplomacy, both of which usually resulted in failure due to European advantages in technology and shifting alliances. Both the colonists and the Native Americans committed atrocities against the other in these conflicts. Many Native Americans captured in war were made slaves; however, the most fatal attack suffered by the Native Americans came in the form of disease. Foreign diseases like small pox ravaged through the Native American population. Some researchers estimate that up to 90% of the Native American population died as a result of foreign diseases brought to America by colonists.

New England Colonies

The New England colonies were New Hampshire, Connecticut, Rhode Island and Massachusetts. These colonies were founded largely to escape **religious persecution** in England. The beliefs of the **Puritans**, who migrated to America in the 1600s, significantly influenced the development of these colonies. Situated in the northeast coastal areas of America, the New England colonies featured numerous harbors as well as dense forests. The soil, however, was rocky and had a very short growing season, so was not well suited for agriculture. The economy of New England during the colonial period centered around fishing, shipbuilding and trade along with some small farms and lumber mills. Although some groups congregated in small farms, life centered mainly in towns and cities where **merchants** largely controlled the trade economy. Coastal cities such as Boston grew and thrived.

> **Review Video: The Massachusetts Bay Colony**
> Visit mometrix.com/academy and enter code: 407058

Middle or Middle Atlantic Colonies

The Middle or Middle Atlantic Colonies were New York, New Jersey, Pennsylvania, and Delaware. Unlike the New England colonies, where most colonists were from England and Scotland, the Middle Colonies founders were from various countries, including the Netherlands and Sweden. Various factors led these colonists to America. More fertile than New England, the Middle Colonies became major producers of **crops**, including rye, oats, potatoes, wheat, and barley. Some particularly wealthy inhabitants owned large farms and/or businesses. Farmers, in general, were able to produce enough to have a surplus to sell. Tenant farmers also rented land from larger landowners.

Southern Colonies

The Southern Colonies were Maryland, Virginia, North Carolina, South Carolina, and Georgia. Of the Southern Colonies, Virginia was the first permanent English colony and Georgia the last. The warm climate and rich soil of the south encouraged **agriculture**, and the growing season was long. As a result, economy in the south was based largely on labor-intensive **plantations**. Crops included tobacco, rice, and indigo, all of which became valuable cash crops. Most land in the south was controlled by wealthy plantation owners and farmers. Labor on the farms came in the form of indentured servants and African slaves. The first of these **African slaves** arrived in Virginia in 1619.

> **Review Video: The Southern Colonies**
> Visit mometrix.com/academy and enter code: 703830
>
> **Review Video: The English Colony of Virginia**
> Visit mometrix.com/academy and enter code: 537399

Significance of the French and Indian Wars

The **British defeat of the Spanish Armada** in 1588 led to the decline of Spanish power in Europe. This, in turn, led the British and French into battle several times between 1689 and 1748. These wars were:

- King William's War, or the Nine Years War, 1689-1697. This war was fought largely in Flanders.
- The War of Spanish Succession, or Queen Anne's War, 1702-1713
- War of Austrian Succession, or King George's War, 1740-1748

The fourth and final war, the **French and Indian War** (1754-1763), was fought largely in the North American territory and resulted in the end of France's reign as a colonial power in North America. Although the French held many advantages, including more cooperative colonists and numerous Native American allies, the strong leadership of **William Pitt** eventually led the British to victory. Costs incurred during the wars eventually led to discontent in the colonies and helped spark the **American Revolution**.

> **Review Video: French and Indian Wars**
> Visit mometrix.com/academy and enter code: 502183

Navigation Acts

The Navigation Acts, enacted in 1651, were an attempt by Britain to dominate international trade. Aimed largely at the Dutch, the acts banned foreign ships from transporting goods to the British colonies and from transporting goods to Britain from elsewhere in Europe. While the restrictions on trade angered some colonists, these acts were helpful to other American colonists who, as members of the British Empire, were legally able to provide ships for Britain's growing trade interests and use the ships for their own trading ventures. By the time the French and Indian War had ended, one-third of British merchant ships were built in the American colonies. Many colonists amassed fortunes in the shipbuilding trade.

Acts of British Parliament that Occurred After the French and Indian Wars

After the French and Indian Wars, the British Parliament passed four major acts:

1. The **Sugar Act**, 1764—this act not only required taxes to be collected on molasses brought into the colonies but gave British officials the right to search the homes of anyone suspected of violating it.

2. The **Stamp Act**, 1765—this act taxed printed materials such as newspapers and legal documents. Protests led the Stamp Act to be repealed in 1766, but the repeal also included the Declaratory Act, which stated that Parliament had the right to govern the colonies.
3. The **Quartering Act**, 1765—this act required colonists to provide accommodations and supplies for British troops. In addition, colonists were prohibited from settling west of the Appalachians until given permission by Britain.
4. The **Townshend Acts**, 1767—these acts taxed paper, paint, lead, and tea that came into the colonies. Colonists led boycotts in protest, and in Massachusetts leaders like Samuel and John Adams began to organize resistance against British rule.

Britain's Taxation of the American Colonies After the French and Indian War

The French and Indian War created circumstances for which the British desperately needed more revenue. These needs included:

- Paying off the war debt
- Defending the expanding empire
- Governing Britain's 33 far-flung colonies, including the American colonies

To meet these needs, the British passed additional laws, increasing revenues from the colonies. Because they had spent so much money to defend the American colonies, the British felt it was appropriate to collect considerably higher **taxes** from them. The colonists felt this was unfair, and many were led to protest the increasing taxes. Eventually, protest led to violence.

Triangular Trade

Triangular trade began in the colonies with ships setting off for **Africa**, carrying rum. In Africa, the rum was traded for gold or slaves. Ships then went from Africa to the **West Indies**, trading slaves for sugar, molasses, or money. To complete the triangle, the ships returned to the **colonies** with sugar or molasses to make more rum, as well as stores of gold and silver. This trade triangle violated the Molasses Act of 1733, which required the colonists to pay high duties to Britain on molasses acquired from French, Dutch, and Spanish colonies. The colonists ignored these duties, and the British government adopted a policy of salutary neglect by not enforcing them.

Review Video: The Triangular Trade
Visit mometrix.com/academy and enter code: 415470

Effects of New Laws on British-Colonial Relations

While earlier revenue-generating acts such as the Navigation Acts brought money to the colonists, the new laws after 1763 required colonists to pay money back to **Britain**. The British felt this was fair since the colonists were British subjects and since they had incurred debt protecting the Colonies. The colonists felt it was not only unfair but illegal.

The development of **local government** in America had given the colonists a different view of the structure and role of government. This made it difficult for the British to understand the colonists' protests against what the British felt was a fair and reasonable solution to the mother country's financial problems.

Factors that Led to Increasing Discontent in the American Colonies

More and more colonists were born on American soil, decreasing any sense of kinship with the far-away British rulers. Their new environment had led to new ideas of government and a strong view of the colonies as a separate entity from Britain. Colonists were allowed to **self-govern** in domestic issues, but **Britain** controlled international issues. In fact, the American colonies were largely left to form their own local government bodies, giving them more freedom than any other colonial territory. This gave the colonists a sense of **independence**, which led them to resent control from Britain. Threats during the French and Indian War led the colonists to call for unification in order to protect themselves.

Colonial and British Government Differences That Caused Tension

As new towns and other legislative districts developed in America, the colonists began to practice **representative government**. Colonial legislative bodies were made up of elected representatives chosen by male property owners in the districts. These individuals represented the interests of the districts from which they had been elected.

By contrast, in Britain, the **Parliament** represented the entire country. Parliament was not elected to represent individual districts. Instead, they represented specific classes. Because of this drastically different approach to government, the British did not understand the colonists' statement that they had no representation in the British Parliament.

Factors that Led to the Boston Massacre

With the passage of the **Stamp Act**, nine colonies met in New York to demand its repeal. Elsewhere, protest arose in New York City, Philadelphia, Boston, and other cities. These protests sometimes escalated into violence, often targeting ruling British officials. The passage of the **Townshend Acts** in 1767 led to additional tension in the colonies. The British sent troops to New York City and Boston. On March 5, 1770, protesters began to taunt the British troops, throwing snowballs. The soldiers responded by firing into the crowd. This clash between protesters and soldiers led to five deaths and eight injuries, and was christened the **Boston Massacre**. Shortly thereafter, Britain repealed the majority of the Townshend Acts.

Tea Act that Led to the Boston Tea Party

The majority of the **Townshend Acts** were repealed after the Boston Massacre in 1770, but Britain kept the tax on tea. In 1773, the **Tea Act** was passed. This allowed the East India Company to sell tea for much lower prices and also allowed them to bypass American distributors, selling directly to shopkeepers instead. Colonial tea merchants saw this as a direct assault on their business. In December of 1773, the **Sons of Liberty** boarded ships in Boston Harbor and dumped 342 chests of tea into the sea in protest of the new laws. This act of protest came to be known as the **Boston Tea Party**.

Coercive Acts Passed after the Boston Tea Party

The Coercive Acts passed by Britain in 1774 were meant to punish Massachusetts for defying British authority. These became collectively known as the **Intolerable Acts** in the colonies and mandated the following:

- Shut down ports in Boston until the city paid back the value of the tea destroyed during the Boston Tea Party
- Required that local government officials in Massachusetts be appointed by the governor rather than being elected by the people
- Allowed trials of British soldiers to be transferred to Britain rather than being held in Massachusetts
- Required locals to provide lodging for British soldiers any time there was a disturbance, even if lodging required them to stay in private homes

These acts led to the assembly of the First Continental Congress in Philadelphia on September 5, 1774. Fifty-five delegates met, representing 12 of the American colonies. They sought compromise with England over England's increasingly harsh efforts to control the colonies.

First Continental Congress

The goal of the First Continental Congress was to achieve a peaceful agreement with Britain. Made up of delegates from 12 of the 13 colonies, the Congress affirmed loyalty to Britain and the power of Parliament to dictate foreign affairs in the colonies. However, they demanded that the **Intolerable Acts** be repealed, and instituted a trade embargo with Britain until this came to pass.

In response, George III of England declared that the American colonies must submit or face military action. The British sought to end assemblies that opposed their policies. These assemblies gathered weapons and began to form militias. On April 19, 1775, the British military was ordered to disperse a meeting of the Massachusetts Assembly. A battle ensued on Lexington Common as the armed colonists resisted. The resulting battles became the **Battle of Lexington and Concord**—the first battles of the **American Revolution**.

Significance of the Second Continental Congress

The Second Continental Congress met in Philadelphia on May 10, 1775, a month after Lexington and Concord. Their discussions centered on the defense of the American colonies and how to conduct the growing war, as well as local government. The delegates also discussed declaring independence from Britain, with many members in favor of this drastic move. They established an army, and on June 15, named **George Washington** as its commander in chief. By 1776, it was obvious that there was no turning back from full-scale war with Britain. The colonial delegates of the Continental Congress signed the **Declaration of Independence** on July 4, 1776.

Review Video: The First and Second Continental Congress
Visit mometrix.com/academy and enter code: 835211

Origins and Basic Ideas of the Declaration of Independence

Penned by Thomas Jefferson and signed on July 4, 1776, the **Declaration of Independence** stated that King George III had violated the rights of the colonists and was establishing a tyrannical reign over them. Many of Jefferson's ideas of natural rights and property rights were shaped by 17th-century philosopher **John Locke**. Jefferson asserted all people's rights to "life, liberty and the pursuit of happiness." Locke's comparable idea asserted "life, liberty, and private property." Both felt that the purpose of government was to protect the rights of the people, and that individual rights were more important than individuals' obligations to the state.

Review Video: Declaration of Independence
Visit mometrix.com/academy and enter code: 256838

Battles of the Revolutionary War

The following are five major battles of the Revolutionary War and their significance:

- The **Battle of Lexington and Concord** (April 1775) is considered the first engagement of the Revolutionary War.
- The **Battle of Bunker Hill** (June 1775) was one of the bloodiest of the entire war. Although American troops withdrew, about half of the British army was lost. The colonists proved they could stand against professional British soldiers. In August, Britain declared that the American colonies were officially in a state of rebellion.

- The first colonial victory occurred in Trenton, New Jersey, when Washington and his troops **crossed the Delaware River** on Christmas Day, 1776, for a December 26 surprise attack on British and Hessian troops.
- The **Battle of Saratoga** effectively ended a plan to separate the New England colonies from their Southern counterparts. The surrender of British general John Burgoyne led to France joining the war as allies of the Americans and is generally considered a turning point of the war.
- On October 19, 1781, General Cornwallis surrendered after a defeat in the **Battle of Yorktown**, ending the Revolutionary War.

Review Video: The American Revolutionary War
Visit mometrix.com/academy and enter code: 935282

Significance of the Treaty of Paris

The Treaty of Paris was signed on September 3, 1783, bringing an official end to the Revolutionary War. In this document, Britain officially recognized the United States of America as an **independent nation**. The treaty established the Mississippi River as the country's western border. The treaty also restored Florida to Spain, while France reclaimed African and Caribbean colonies seized by the British in 1763. On November 25, 1783, the last British troops departed from the newly born United States of America.

Significance of the Articles of Confederation

A precursor to the Constitution, the **Articles of Confederation** represented the first attempt of the newly independent colonies to establish the basics of government. The Continental Congress approved the Articles on November 15, 1777. They went into effect on March 1, 1781, following ratification by the thirteen states. The articles prevented a central government from gaining too much power, instead giving power to a **congressional body** made up of **delegates** from all thirteen states. However, the individual states retained final authority.

Without a strong central **executive**, though, this weak alliance among the new states proved ineffective in settling disputes or enforcing laws. The idea of a weak central government needed to be revised. Recognition of these weaknesses eventually led to the drafting of a new document, the **Constitution**.

Review Video: Articles of Confederation
Visit mometrix.com/academy and enter code: 927401

Initial Proposition and Draft of the Constitution

Delegates from twelve of the thirteen states (Rhode Island was not represented) met in Philadelphia in May of 1787, initially intending to revise the Articles of Confederation. However, it quickly became apparent that a simple revision would not provide the workable governmental structure the newly formed country needed. After vowing to keep all the proceedings secret until the final document was completed, the delegates set out to draft what would eventually become the **Constitution of the United States of America**. By keeping the negotiations secret, the delegates were able to present a completed document to the country for ratification, rather than having every small detail hammered out by the general public.

General Structure of Government Proposed by the Delegates

The delegates agreed that the new nation required a **strong central government** but that its overall power should be **limited**. The various branches of the government should have **balanced**

power, so that no one group could control the others. Final power belonged to the **citizens** who voted officials into office based on who would provide the best representation.

Objections Against the Constitution

Once the Constitution was drafted, it was presented for approval by the states. Nine states needed to approve the document for it to become official. However, debate and discussion continued. Major **concerns** included:

- There was no bill of rights to protect individual freedoms.
- States felt too much power was being handed over to the central government.
- Voters wanted more control over their elected representatives.

Discussion about necessary changes to the Constitution was divided into two camps: Federalists and Anti-Federalists. **Federalists** wanted a strong central government. **Anti-Federalists** wanted to prevent a tyrannical government from developing if a central government held too much power

Major Players in the Federalist and Anti-Federalist camps

Major Federalist leaders included Alexander Hamilton, John Jay, and James Madison. They wrote a series of letters, called the **Federalist Papers**, aimed at convincing the states to ratify the Constitution. These were published in New York papers. Anti-Federalists included Thomas Jefferson and Patrick Henry. They argued against the Constitution as it was originally drafted in a series of **Anti-Federalist Papers**.

The final compromise produced a strong central government controlled by checks and balances. A **Bill of Rights** was also added, becoming the first ten amendments to the Constitution. These amendments protected rights such as freedom of speech, freedom of religion, and other basic rights. Aside from various amendments added throughout the years, the United States Constitution has remained unchanged.

Individuals Who Formed the First Administration of the New Government

The individuals who formed the first administration of the new government were:

- **George Washington**—elected as the first President of the United States in 1789
- **John Adams**—finished second in the election and became the first Vice President
- **Thomas Jefferson**—appointed by Washington as Secretary of State
- **Alexander Hamilton**—appointed Secretary of the Treasury

The Virginia Plan, the New Jersey Plan, and the Great Compromise

Disagreement immediately occurred between delegates from large states and those from smaller states. James Madison and Edmund Randolph (the governor of Virginia) felt that representation in Congress should be based on state population. This was the **Virginia Plan**. The **New Jersey Plan**, presented by William Paterson from New Jersey, proposed that each state should have equal representation. Finally, Roger Sherman from Connecticut formulated the **Connecticut Compromise**, also called the Great Compromise. The result was the familiar structure we have today. Each state has the equal representation of two Senators in the Senate, with the number of representatives in the House of Representatives based on population. This is called a **bicameral congress**. Both houses may draft bills, but financial matters must originate in the House of Representatives.

THE THREE-FIFTHS COMPROMISE AND NUMBER OF REPRESENTATIVES FOR EACH STATE

During debate on the US Constitution, a disagreement arose between the Northern and Southern states involving how **slaves** should be counted when determining a state's quota of representatives. In the South, large numbers of slaves were commonly used to run plantations. Delegates wanted slaves to be counted to determine the number of representatives but not counted to determine the amount of taxes the states would pay. The Northern states wanted exactly the opposite arrangement. The final decision was to count three-fifths of the slave population both for tax purposes and to determine representation. This was called the **Three-fifths Compromise**.

PROVISIONS OF THE COMMERCE COMPROMISE

The Commerce Compromise also resulted from a North/South disagreement. In the North, the economy was centered on **industry and trade**. The Southern economy was largely **agricultural**. The Northern states wanted to give the new government the ability to regulate exports as well as trade between the states. The South opposed this plan. Another compromise was in order. In the end, Congress received regulatory power over all trade, including the ability to collect **tariffs** on exported goods. In the South, this raised another red flag regarding the slave trade, as they were concerned about the effect on their economy if tariffs were levied on slaves. The final agreement allowed importing slaves to continue for twenty years without government intervention. Import taxes on slaves were limited, and after the year 1808, Congress could decide whether to allow continued imports of slaves.

American History 1790 to 1898

ALIEN AND SEDITION ACTS

When **John Adams** became president, a war was raging between Britain and France. While Adams and the Federalists backed the British, Thomas Jefferson and the Democratic-Republican Party supported the French. The United States nearly went to war with France during this time period, while France worked to spread its international standing and influence under the leadership of **Napoleon Bonaparte**. The **Alien and Sedition Acts** grew out of this conflict and made it illegal to speak in a hostile fashion against the existing government. They also allowed the president to deport anyone in the US who was not a citizen and who was suspected of treason or treasonous activity. When Jefferson became the third president in 1800, he repealed these four laws and pardoned anyone who had been convicted under them.

DEVELOPMENT OF POLITICAL PARTIES IN EARLY US GOVERNMENT

Many in the US were against political parties after seeing the way parties, or factions, functioned in Britain. The factions in Britain were more interested in personal profit than the overall good of the country, and they did not want this to happen in the US.

However, the differences of opinion between Thomas Jefferson and Alexander Hamilton led to the formation of **political parties**. Hamilton favored a stronger central government, while Jefferson felt that more power should remain with the states. Jefferson was in favor of strict Constitutional interpretation, while Hamilton believed in a more flexible approach. As others joined the two camps, Hamilton backers began to call themselves **Federalists**, while those supporting Jefferson became identified as **Democratic-Republicans**.

Development of the Whig, the Democratic, and the Republican Parties

Thomas Jefferson was elected president in 1800 and again in 1804. The **Federalist Party** began to decline, and its major figure, Alexander Hamilton, died in a duel with Aaron Burr in 1804. By 1816, the Federalist Party had virtually disappeared.

New parties sprang up to take its place. After 1824, the **Democratic-Republican Party** suffered a split. The **Whigs** rose, backing John Quincy Adams and industrial growth. The new Democratic Party formed in opposition to the Whigs, and their candidate, Andrew Jackson, was elected as president in 1828.

By the 1850s, issues regarding slavery led to the formation of the **Republican Party**, which was anti-slavery, while the Democratic Party, with a larger interest in the South, favored slavery. This Republican/Democrat division formed the basis of today's **two-party system**.

Significance of Marbury v. Madison

The main duty of the Supreme Court today is **judicial review**. This power was largely established by **Marbury v. Madison**. When John Adams was voted out of office in 1800, he worked during his final days in office to appoint Federalist judges to Supreme Court positions, knowing Jefferson, his replacement, held opposing views. As late as March 3, the day before Jefferson was to take office, Adams made last-minute appointments referred to as "Midnight Judges." One of the late appointments was William Marbury. The next day, March 4, Jefferson ordered his Secretary of State, James Madison, not to deliver Marbury's commission. This decision was backed by Chief Justice Marshall, who determined that the **Judiciary Act of 1789**, which granted the power to deliver commissions, was illegal in that it gave the Judicial Branch powers not granted in the Constitution. This case set precedent for the Supreme Court to nullify laws it found to be **unconstitutional**.

Review Video: Marbury v Madison
Visit mometrix.com/academy and enter code: 573964

Political Motivations Behind France Selling the Louisiana Purchase

With tension still high between France and Britain, Napoleon was in need of money to support his continuing war efforts. To secure necessary funds, he decided to sell the **Louisiana Territory** to the US. President **Thomas Jefferson** wanted to buy New Orleans, feeling US trade was made vulnerable to both Spain and France at that port. Instead, Napoleon sold him the entire territory for the bargain price of $15 million. The Louisiana Territory was larger than all the rest of the United States put together, and it eventually became 15 additional states.

Federalists in Congress were opposed to the purchase. They feared that the Louisiana Purchase would extend slavery, and that further western growth would weaken the power of the northern states.

Lewis and Clark Expedition

The purchase of the **Louisiana Territory** from France in 1803 more than doubled the size of the United States. President Thomas Jefferson wanted to have the area mapped and explored, since much of the territory was wilderness. He chose Meriwether Lewis and William Clark to head an expedition into the Louisiana Territory. After two years, Lewis and Clark returned, having traveled all the way to the Pacific Ocean. They brought maps, detailed journals, and a multitude of information about the wide expanse of land they had traversed. The **Lewis and Clark Expedition** opened up the west in the Louisiana Territory and beyond for further exploration and settlement.

> **Review Video: Purpose of the Lewis and Clark Expedition**
> Visit mometrix.com/academy and enter code: 570657

Causes and Result of the War of 1812

The War of 1812 grew out of the continuing tension between France and Great Britain. Napoleon continued striving to conquer Britain, while the US continued trade with both countries but favored France and the French colonies. Because of what Britain saw as an alliance between America and France, they determined to bring an end to trade between the two nations.

With the British preventing US trade with the French and the French preventing trade with the British, James Madison's presidency introduced acts to **regulate international trade**. If either Britain or France removed their restrictions, America would not trade with the other country. Napoleon acted first, and Madison prohibited trade with England. England saw this as the US formally siding with the French, and war ensued in 1812.

The **War of 1812** has been called the **Second American Revolution**. It established the superiority of the US naval forces and reestablished US independence from Britain and Europe.

The British had two major objections to America's continued trade with France. First, they saw the US as helping France's war effort by providing supplies and goods. Second, the United States had grown into a competitor, taking trade and money away from British ships and tradesmen. In its attempts to end American trade with France, the British put into effect the **Orders in Council**, which made any and all French-owned ports off-limits to American ships. They also began to seize American ships and conscript their crews.

> **Review Video: Overview of the War of 1812**
> Visit mometrix.com/academy and enter code: 507716
>
> **Review Video: Opinions About the War of 1812**
> Visit mometrix.com/academy and enter code: 274558

Major Military Events of the War of 1812

Two major naval battles, at **Lake Erie** and **Lake Champlain**, kept the British from invading the US via Canada. American attempts to conquer Canadian lands were not successful.

In another memorable British attack, the British invaded Washington, DC and burned the White House on August 24, 1814. Legend has it that **Dolley Madison**, the First Lady, salvaged the portrait of George Washington from the fire. On Christmas Eve, 1814, the **Treaty of Ghent** officially ended the war. However, Andrew Jackson, unaware that the war was over, managed another victory at New Orleans on January 8, 1815. This victory improved American morale and led to a new wave of national pride and support known as the "**Era of Good Feelings**."

Influence of the American System on American Economics

Spurred by the trade conflicts of the War of 1812 and supported by Henry Clay among others, the **American System** set up tariffs to help protect American interests from competition with overseas products. Reducing competition led to growth in employment and an overall increase in American industry. The higher tariffs also provided funds for the government to pay for various improvements. Congress passed high tariffs in 1816 and also chartered a federal bank. The **Second Bank of the United States** was given the job of regulating America's money supply.

McCulloch v. Maryland

Judicial review was further exercised by the Supreme Court in **McCulloch v. Maryland**. When Congress chartered a national bank, the **Second Bank of the United States**, Maryland voted to tax any bank business dealing with banks chartered outside the state, including the federally chartered bank. Andrew McCulloch, an employee of the Second Bank of the US in Baltimore, refused to pay this tax. The resulting lawsuit from the State of Maryland went to the Supreme Court for judgment.

John Marshall, Chief Justice of the Supreme Court, stated that Congress was within its rights to charter a national bank. In addition, the State of Maryland did not have the power to levy a tax on the federal bank or on the federal government in general. In cases where state and federal government collided, precedent was set for the **federal government** to prevail.

Effects of the Missouri Compromise on the Tensions Between the North and South

By 1819, the United States had developed a tenuous balance between slave and free states, with exactly 22 senators in Congress from each faction. However, Missouri was ready to join the union. As a slave state, it would tip the balance in Congress. To prevent this imbalance, the **Missouri Compromise** brought the northern part of Massachusetts into the union as Maine, establishing it as a free state to balance the admission of Missouri as a slave state. In addition, the remaining portion of the Louisiana Purchase was to remain free north of **latitude 36°30'**. Since cotton did not grow well this far north, this limitation was acceptable to congressmen representing the slave states.

However, the proposed Missouri constitution presented a problem, as it outlawed immigration of free blacks into the state. Another compromise was in order, this time proposed by **Henry Clay**. According to this new compromise, Missouri would never pass a law that prevented anyone from entering the state. Through this and other work, Clay earned his title of the "**Great Compromiser**."

Review Video: The Missouri Compromise
Visit mometrix.com/academy and enter code: 848091

Monroe Doctrine

On December 2, 1823, President Monroe delivered a message to Congress in which he introduced the **Monroe Doctrine**. In this address, he stated that any attempts by European powers to establish new colonies on the North American continent would be considered interference in American politics. The US would stay out of European matters, and expected Europe to offer America the same courtesy. This approach to foreign policy stated in no uncertain terms that America would not tolerate any new European colonies in the New World, and that events occurring in Europe would no longer influence the policies and doctrines of the US.

Review Video: What was the Monroe Doctrine?
Visit mometrix.com/academy and enter code: 953021

Effect of the Treaty of Paris on Native Americans

After the Revolutionary War, the **Treaty of Paris**, which outlined the terms of surrender of the British to the Americans, granted large parcels of land to the US that were occupied by Native Americans. The new government attempted to claim the land, treating the natives as a conquered people. This approach proved unenforceable.

Next, the government tried purchasing the land from the Native Americans via a series of **treaties** as the country expanded westward. In practice, however, these treaties were not honored, and Native Americans were simply dislocated and forced to move farther and farther west, often with military action, as American expansion continued.

Indian Removal Act of 1830 and the Treaty of New Echota

The Indian Removal Act of 1830 gave the new American government power to form treaties with Native Americans. In theory, America would claim land east of the Mississippi in exchange for land west of the Mississippi, to which the natives would relocate voluntarily. In practice, many tribal leaders were forced into signing the treaties, and relocation at times occurred by force.

The **Treaty of New Echota** in 1835 was supposedly a treaty between the US government and Cherokee tribes in Georgia. However, the treaty was not signed by tribal leaders but rather by a small portion of the represented people. The leaders protested and refused to leave, but President Martin Van Buren enforced the treaty by sending soldiers. During their forced relocation, more than 4,000 Cherokees died on what became known as the **Trail of Tears**.

Review Video: Indian Removal Act
Visit mometrix.com/academy and enter code: 666738

Jacksonian Democracy vs. Preceding Political Climate

Jacksonian Democracy is largely seen as a shift from politics favoring the wealthy to politics favoring the common man. The right to vote was given to all free white males, not just property owners, as had been the case previously. Jackson's approach favored the patronage system, laissez-faire economics, and relocation of the Native American tribes from the Southeast portion of the country. Jackson opposed the formation of a federal bank and allowed the Second Bank of the United States to collapse by vetoing a bill to renew the charter. Jackson also faced the challenge of the **Nullification Crisis** when South Carolina claimed that it could ignore or nullify any federal law it considered unconstitutional. Jackson sent troops to the state to enforce the protested tariff laws, and a compromise engineered by Henry Clay in 1833 settled the matter for the time being.

Second Great Awakening

Led by Protestant evangelical leaders, the **Second Great Awakening** occurred between 1800 and 1830. Several missionary groups grew out of the movement, including the **American Home Missionary Society**, which formed in 1826. The ideas behind the Second Great Awakening focused on personal responsibility, both as an individual and in response to injustice and suffering. The **American Bible Society** and the **American Tract Society** provided literature, while various traveling preachers spread the word. New denominations arose, including the Latter-day Saints and Seventh-day Adventists.

Another movement associated with the Second Great Awakening was the **temperance movement**, focused on ending the production and use of alcohol. One major organization behind the temperance movement was the **Society for the Promotion of Temperance**, formed in 1826 in Boston.

Attitudes Toward Education in the Early 19th Century

Horace Mann, among others, felt that schools could help children become better citizens, keep them away from crime, prevent poverty, and help American society become more unified. His *Common School Journal* brought his ideas of the importance of education into the public consciousness and proposed his suggestions for an improved American education system.

Increased literacy led to increased awareness of current events, Western expansion, and other major developments of the time period. Public interest and participation in the arts and literature also increased. By the end of the 19th century, all children had access to a **free public elementary education**.

Development of Economic Trends as the US Continued to Grow

In the Northeast, the economy mostly depended on **manufacturing, industry, and industrial development**. This led to a dichotomy between rich business owners and industrial leaders and the much poorer workers who supported their businesses. The South continued to depend on **agriculture**, especially on large-scale farms or plantations worked mostly by slaves and indentured servants. In the West, where new settlements had begun to develop, the land was largely wild. Growing communities were essentially **agricultural**, raising crops and livestock. The differences between regions led each to support different interests both politically and economically.

Industrial Activity Before and After 1800

During the 18th century, goods were often manufactured in houses or small shops. With increased technology allowing for the use of machines, **factories** began to develop. In factories, a large volume of salable goods could be produced in a much shorter amount of time. Many Americans, including increasing numbers of **immigrants**, found jobs in these factories, which were in constant need of labor. Another major invention was the **cotton gin**, which significantly decreased the processing time of cotton and was a major factor in the rapid expansion of cotton production in the South.

Development of Labor Movements in the 1800s

In 1751, a group of bakers held a protest in which they stopped baking bread. This was technically the first American **labor strike**. In the 1830s and 1840s, labor movements began in earnest. Boston's masons, carpenters, and stoneworkers protested the length of the workday, fighting to reduce it to ten hours. In 1844, a group of women in the textile industry also fought to reduce their workday to ten hours, forming the **Lowell Female Labor Reform Association**. Many other protests occurred and organizations developed through this time period with the same goal in mind.

Major Ideas Driving American Foreign Policy

The three major ideas driving American foreign policy during its early years were:

- **Isolationism**—the early US government did not intend to establish colonies, though they did plan to grow larger within the bounds of North America.
- **No entangling alliances**—both George Washington and Thomas Jefferson were opposed to forming any permanent alliances with other countries or becoming involved in other countries' internal issues.
- **Nationalism**—a positive patriotic feeling about the United States blossomed quickly among its citizens, particularly after the War of 1812, when the US once again defeated Britain. The Industrial Revolution also sparked increased nationalism by allowing even the most far-flung areas of the US to communicate with each other via telegraph and the expanding railroad.

Effects of Manifest Destiny on American Politics

In the 1800s, many believed America was destined by God to expand west, bringing as much of the North American continent as possible under the umbrella of the US government. With the Northwest Ordinance and the Louisiana Purchase, over half of the continent became American.

However, the rapid and relentless expansion brought conflict with the Native Americans, Great Britain, Mexico, and Spain. One result of "**Manifest Destiny**" was the **Mexican-American War** from 1846 to 1848. By the end of the war, Texas, California, and a large portion of what is now the American Southwest joined the growing nation. Conflict also arose over the **Oregon Territory**, shared by the US and Britain. In 1846, President James Polk resolved this problem by compromising with Britain, establishing a US boundary south of the 49th parallel.

Review Video: Manifest Destiny
Visit mometrix.com/academy and enter code: 957409

Mexican-American War

Spain had held colonial interests in America since the 1540s—earlier even than Great Britain. In 1810, **Mexico** revolted against Spain, becoming a free nation in 1821. **Texas** followed suit, declaring its independence after an 1836 revolution. In 1844, the Democrats pressed President Tyler to annex Texas. Unlike his predecessor, Andrew Jackson, Tyler agreed to admit Texas into the Union, and in 1845, Texas became a state.

During Mexico's war for independence, the nation incurred $4.5 million in war debts to the US. Newly elected James K. Polk offered to forgive the debts in return for New Mexico and Upper California, but Mexico refused. In 1846, war was declared in response to a Mexican attack on American troops that President Polk had moved into a disputed zone between the Rio Grande and Nueces River. As US victory grew more certain, dispute arose over how to handle slavery in any newly acquired territory. The **Wilmot Proviso**, though it was never passed, was a large source of contention, as it aimed to prohibit slavery in any territory acquired from Mexico—sowing further seeds of tension between the North and the South. The Mexican-American War ended in 1848 with Mexico agreeing to sell California and its remaining territory north of the Rio Grande.

Review Video: The Mexican-American War
Visit mometrix.com/academy and enter code: 271216

Review Video: Sectional Crisis: The Wilmot Proviso
Visit mometrix.com/academy and enter code: 974842

Popular Sovereignty and the Compromise of 1850

In addition to the pro-slavery and anti-slavery factions, a third group rose, who felt that each individual state should decide whether to allow or permit slavery within its borders. The idea that a state could make its own choices was referred to as **popular sovereignty**.

When California applied to join the union in 1849, the balance of congressional power was again threatened. The **Compromise of 1850** introduced a group of laws meant to bring an end to the conflict:

- California's admittance as a free state
- The outlaw of the slave trade in Washington, DC
- An increase in efforts to capture escaped slaves
- The right of New Mexico and Utah territories to decide individually whether to allow slavery

In spite of these measures, debate raged each time a new state prepared to enter the union.

Gadsden Purchase and the 1853 Post-War Treaty with Mexico

After the Mexican-American war, a **second treaty** in 1853 determined hundreds of miles of America's southwest borders. In 1854, the **Gadsden Purchase** was finalized, providing even more territory to aid in the building of the transcontinental railroad. This purchase added what would eventually become the southernmost regions of Arizona and New Mexico to the growing nation. The modern outline of the United States was by this time nearly complete.

Kansas-Nebraska Act Trigger of Additional Conflict

With the creation of the Kansas and Nebraska territories in 1854, another debate began. Congress allowed popular sovereignty in these territories, but slavery opponents argued that the Missouri Compromise had already made slavery illegal in this region. In Kansas, two separate governments arose, one pro-slavery and one anti-slavery. Conflict between the two factions rose to violence, leading Kansas to gain the nickname of "**Bleeding Kansas**."

Review Video: Sectional Crisis: The Kansas-Nebraska Act
Visit mometrix.com/academy and enter code: 982119

Early Leaders in the Women's Rights Movement

The women's rights movement began in the 1840s, with leaders including Elizabeth Cady Stanton, Sojourner Truth, Ernestine Rose, and Lucretia Mott. In 1869, Elizabeth Cady Stanton and Susan B. Anthony formed the **National Woman Suffrage Association**, fighting for women's right to vote.

In 1848, in Seneca Falls, the first women's rights convention was held, with about 300 attendees. The two-day **Seneca Falls Convention** discussed the rights of women to vote (suffrage) as well as equal treatment in careers, legal proceedings, etc. The convention produced a "Declaration of Sentiments," which outlined a plan for women to attain the rights they deserved. **Frederick Douglass** supported the women's rights movement, as well as the abolition movement. In fact, women's rights and abolition movements often went hand-in-hand during this time period.

Review Video: The Women's Rights Movement in America
Visit mometrix.com/academy and enter code: 987734

Events and Developments that Brought the North and South into Conflict

The conflict between the North and South coalesced around the issue of **slavery**, but other elements contributed to the growing disagreement. Though most farmers in the South worked small farms with little or no slave labor, the huge plantations run by the South's rich depended on slaves or indentured servants to remain profitable. They had also become more dependent on **cotton**, with slave populations growing in concert with the rapid increase in cotton production. In the North, a more diverse agricultural economy and the growth of **industry** made slaves rarer. The **abolitionist movement** grew steadily, with Harriet Beecher Stowe's *Uncle Tom's Cabin* giving many an idea to rally around. A collection of anti-slavery organizations formed, with many actively working to free slaves in the South, often bringing them to the northern states or Canada.

Dred Scott Decision

Abolitionist factions coalesced around the case of **Dred Scott**, using his case to test the country's laws regarding slavery. Scott, a slave, had been taken by his owner from Missouri, which was a slave state. He then traveled to Illinois, a free state, then on to the Minnesota Territory, also free based on the Missouri Compromise. After several years, he returned to Missouri, and his owner subsequently died. Abolitionists took Scott's case to court, stating that Scott was no longer a slave but free, since he had lived in free territory. The case went to the Supreme Court.

The Supreme Court stated that, because Scott, as a slave, was not a US citizen, his time in free states did not change his status. He also did not have the right to sue. In addition, the Court determined that the **Missouri Compromise** was unconstitutional, stating that Congress had overstepped its bounds by outlawing slavery in the territories.

Review Video: The Dred Scott Act
Visit mometrix.com/academy and enter code: 364838

Anti-Slavery Organizations

Five anti-slavery organizations and their significance are:

- **American Colonization Society**—Protestant churches formed this group, aimed at returning black slaves to Africa. Former slaves subsequently formed Liberia, but the colony did not do well, as the region was not well-suited for agriculture.
- **American Anti-Slavery Society**—William Lloyd Garrison, a Quaker, was the major force behind this group and its newspaper, *The Liberator*.
- **Philadelphia Female Anti-Slavery Society**—this women-only group was formed by Margaretta Forten because women were not allowed to join the Anti-Slavery Society formed by her father.
- **Anti-Slavery Convention of American Women**—this group continued meeting even after pro-slavery factions burned down their original meeting place.
- **Female Vigilant Society**—this organization raised funds to help the Underground Railroad, as well as slave refugees.

Incidents at Harper's Ferry and John Brown's Role

John Brown, an abolitionist, had participated in several anti-slavery activities, including killing five pro-slavery men in retaliation, after the sacking of Lawrence, Kansas, an anti-slavery town. He and other abolitionists also banded together to pool their funds and build a runaway slave colony.

In 1859, Brown seized a federal arsenal in **Harper's Ferry**, located in what is now West Virginia. Brown intended to seize guns and ammunition and lead a slave rebellion. **Robert E. Lee** captured Brown and 21 followers, who were subsequently tried and hanged. While Northerners took the executions as an indication that the government supported slavery, Southerners were of the opinion that most of the North supported Brown and were, in general, anti-slavery.

Presidential Candidates for the 1860 Election

The 1860 presidential candidates represented four different parties, each with a different opinion on slavery:

- **John Breckinridge**, representing the Southern Democrats, was pro-slavery but urged compromise to preserve the Union.
- **Abraham Lincoln**, of the Republican Party, was anti-slavery.
- **Stephen Douglas**, of the Northern Democrats, felt that the issue should be determined locally, on a state-by-state basis.
- **John Bell**, of the Constitutional Union Party, focused primarily on keeping the Union intact.

In the end, Abraham Lincoln won both the popular and electoral election. Southern states, who had sworn to secede from the Union if Lincoln was elected, did so, led by South Carolina and followed by the rest of the Deep South (Mississippi, Alabama, Georgia, Louisiana, Florida, and Texas). These states established the **Confederate States of America**, with its capital in Montgomery, Alabama.

The president of the CSA was **Jefferson Davis**. Outgoing US President Buchanan claimed that he had no constitutional authority to stop the secession, but upon entering office, Lincoln attempted to maintain control of all Southern forts. This led to the firing on **Ft. Sumter** (SC) by the Confederates. As Lincoln called for aid, the Upper South (Virginia, Arkansas, North Carolina, and Tennessee) seceded as well, and the CSA made Richmond, Virginia its new capital.

Compromises to Save the Union

The US government made a number of compromises in an attempt to preserve the Union after Lincoln's election. The **Crittenden Compromise** extended the line of the Missouri Compromise and promised federal protection of slavery south of that line. The **House of Representatives Compromise** offered an extension of the Missouri Compromise and a Constitutional amendment to protect slavery. The **Virginia Peace Convention** produced an offer to extend the line of the Missouri Compromise and establish that slavery can never be outlawed except by the permission of the owner. Finally, Congress offered $300 for each slave. The South said that this was not enough money, and the North was appalled by the offer, regardless. It became clear that such compromises would not be enough to save the Union.

North vs. South in the Civil War

The Northern states had significant advantages, including:

- **Larger population**—the North consisted of 24 states, while the South had 11.
- **Better transportation and finances**—with railroads primarily in the North, supply chains were much more dependable, as was overseas trade.
- **Raw materials**—the North held the majority of America's gold, as well as iron, copper, and other minerals vital to wartime.

The South's advantages included the following:

- **Better-trained military officers**—many of the Southern officers were West Point trained and had commanded in the Mexican and Indian wars.
- **Familiarity with weapons**—the climate and lifestyle of the South meant most of the people were experienced with both guns and horses. The industrial North had less extensive experience.
- **Defensive position**—the South felt that victory was guaranteed, since they were protecting their own lands, while the North would be invading.
- **Well-defined goals**—the South fought an ideological war to be allowed to govern themselves and preserve their way of life. The North originally fought to preserve the Union and later to free the slaves.

Review Video: American Civil War: North vs. South Overview
Visit mometrix.com/academy and enter code: 370788

Benefit of the Emancipation Proclamation on the Union's Military Strategy

The Emancipation Proclamation, issued by President Lincoln on January 1, 1863, freed all slaves in **Confederate states** that were still in rebellion against the Union. While the original proclamation did not free any slaves in the states actually under Union control, it did set a precedent for the emancipation of slaves as the war progressed.

The **Emancipation Proclamation** worked in the Union's favor, as many freed slaves and other black troops joined the **Union Army**. Almost 200,000 blacks fought in the Union army, and over

10,000 served in the navy. By the end of the war, over 4 million slaves had been freed, and in 1865 slavery was abolished in the **13th amendment** to the Constitution.

Review Video: The Civil War: The Emancipation Proclamation
Visit mometrix.com/academy and enter code: 181778

Major Events of the Civil War

Six major events of the Civil War and their outcomes or significance are:

- The **First Battle of Bull Run** (July 21, 1861)—this was the first major land battle of the war. Observers, expecting to enjoy an entertaining skirmish, set up picnics nearby. Instead, they found themselves witness to a bloodbath. Union forces were defeated, and the battle set the course of the Civil War as long, bloody, and costly.
- The **Capture of Fort Henry** by Ulysses S. Grant—this battle in February of 1862 marked the Union's first major victory.
- The **Battle of Gettysburg** (July 1-3, 1863)—often seen as the turning point of the war, Gettysburg also saw the largest number of casualties of the war, with over 50,000 dead, wounded, or missing. Robert E. Lee was defeated, and the Confederate army, significantly crippled, withdrew.
- The **Overland Campaign** (May and June of 1864)—Grant, now in command of all the Union armies, led this high casualty campaign that eventually positioned the Union for victory.
- **Sherman's March to the Sea**—William Tecumseh Sherman, in May of 1864, conquered Atlanta. He then continued to Savannah, destroying vast amounts of property as he went.
- Following Lee's defeat at the Appomattox Courthouse, General Grant accepted **Lee's surrender** in the home of Wilmer McLean in Appomattox, Virginia on April 9, 1865.

Impact of the Civil War across America

The Civil War impacted various people in America in remarkable ways. The people most affected were likely African Americans, who were at the center of the divide between the North and the South. Many African Americans directly fought in the war on both sides. Those in the Southern states were ultimately freed as a result of the Emancipation Proclamation of 1863. Soldiers in the war saw brutal warfare and faced physical and psychological repercussions of combat. It has long been said about the Civil War that soldiers often knew or were related to the very people they were fighting. This was especially so in states that hosted battles or lied on the borders between Southern and Northern states, such as Virginia and Tennessee. Others affected included women and children who were, in some cases, located fairly near the fights and played roles as suppliers, medics, and activists, leading to some precursors to the women's rights movement. In the reconstruction, economic, political, legal, and emotional fallout had to be dealt with, leading to many decades of repair following the war.

Circumstances of Lincoln's Assassination

The Civil War ended with the surrender of the South on April 9, 1865. Five days later, Lincoln and his wife, Mary, went to the play *Our American Cousin* at the Ford Theater. John Wilkes Booth, who did not know that the war was over, did his part in a plot to help the Confederacy by shooting Lincoln. He was carried from the theater to a nearby house, where he died the next morning. Booth was tracked down and killed by Union soldiers twelve days later.

Review Video: Overview of the American Civil War
Visit mometrix.com/academy and enter code: 239557

Goals of Reconstruction and the Freedmen's Bureau

In the aftermath of the Civil War, the South was left in chaos. From 1865 to 1877, government on all levels worked to help restore order to the South, ensure civil rights to the freed slaves, and bring the Confederate states back into the Union. This became known as the **Reconstruction period**. In 1866, Congress passed the **Reconstruction Acts**, placing former Confederate states under military rule and stating the grounds for readmission into the Union.

The **Freedmen's Bureau** was formed to help freedmen both with basic necessities like food and clothing and also with employment and finding of family members who had been separated during the war. Many in the South felt the Freedmen's Bureau worked to set freed slaves against their former owners. The Bureau was intended to help former slaves become self-sufficient, and to keep them from falling prey to those who would take advantage of them. It eventually closed due to lack of funding and to violence from the **Ku Klux Klan**.

Policies of the Radical and Moderate Republicans

The **Radical Republicans** wished to treat the South quite harshly after the war. **Thaddeus Stevens**, the House Leader, suggested that the Confederate states be treated as if they were territories again, with ten years of military rule and territorial government before they would be readmitted. He also wanted to give all black men the right to vote. Former Confederate soldiers would be required to swear they had never supported the Confederacy (knows as the "Ironclad Oath") in order to be granted full rights as American citizens.

In contrast, the **moderate Republicans** wanted only black men who were literate or who had served as Union troops to be able to vote. All Confederate soldiers except troop leaders would also be able to vote. Before his death, **Lincoln** had favored a more moderate approach to Reconstruction, hoping this approach might bring some states back into the Union before the end of the war.

Phases of Reconstruction

The three phases of Reconstruction are:

- **Presidential Reconstruction**—largely driven by President Andrew Johnson's policies, the presidential phase of Reconstruction was lenient on the South and allowed continued discrimination against and control over blacks.
- **Congressional Reconstruction**—Congress, controlled largely by Radical Republicans, took a different stance, providing a wider range of civil rights for blacks and greater control over Southern government. Congressional Reconstruction is marked by military control of the former Confederate States.
- **Redemption**—gradually, the Confederate states were readmitted into the Union. During this time, white Democrats took over the government of most of the South. In 1877, President Rutherford Hayes withdrew the last federal troops from the South.

Carpetbaggers and Scalawags

The chaos in the South attracted a number of people seeking to fill the power vacuums and take advantage of the economic disruption. **Scalawags** were southern whites who aligned with freedmen to take over local governments. Many in the South who could have filled political offices refused to take the necessary oath required to grant them the right to vote, leaving many opportunities for Scalawags and others. **Carpetbaggers** were Northerners who traveled to the South for various reasons. Some provided assistance, while others sought to make money or to acquire political power during this chaotic period.

Black Codes and the Civil Rights Bill

The Black Codes were proposed to control freed slaves. They would not be allowed to bear arms, assemble, serve on juries, or testify against whites. Schools would be segregated, and unemployed blacks could be arrested and forced to work. The **Civil Rights Act** countered these codes, providing much wider rights for the freed slaves.

Andrew Johnson, who became president after Lincoln's death, supported the Black Codes and vetoed the Civil Rights Act in 1865 and again in 1866. The second time, Congress overrode his veto, and it became law.

Two years later, Congress voted to **impeach** Johnson, the culmination of tensions between Congress and the president. He was tried and came within a single vote of being convicted, but ultimately was acquitted and finished his term in office.

Purpose of the Thirteenth, Fourteenth, and Fifteenth Amendments

The Thirteenth, Fourteenth and Fifteenth Amendments were all passed shortly after the end of the Civil War:

- The **Thirteenth Amendment** was ratified by the states on December 6, 1865. This amendment prohibited slavery in the United States.
- The **Fourteenth Amendment** overturned the Dred Scott decision and was ratified July 9, 1868. American citizenship was redefined: a citizen was any person born or naturalized in the US, with all citizens guaranteed equal legal protection by all states. It also guaranteed citizens of any race the right to file a lawsuit or serve on a jury.
- The **Fifteenth Amendment** was ratified on February 3, 1870. It states that no citizen of the United States can be denied the right to vote based on race, color, or previous status as a slave.

Black Southerners and Segregation

Most Southern Democrats supported **segregation**, or the separation of the races. Although the **Civil Rights Act of 1875** had outlawed segregated restaurants and hotels, among other things, the Supreme Court ruled in 1883 that this act violated the 14th amendment because only states, and not individuals, could be forbidden from segregation. The **Jim Crow laws** were those rules that segregated black people and white people. Although de facto (by custom) segregation had existed in the North for years, the South began to implement segregation de jure (by law). In **Plessy v. Ferguson** (1896), the Supreme Court ruled that accommodations should be "separate but equal." In **Cummings v. Board of Education** (1898), the Supreme Court allowed public schools to be segregated.

Developments in Transportation

As America expanded its borders, it also developed new technology to travel the rapidly growing country. Roads and railroads traversed the nation, with the **Transcontinental Railroad** eventually allowing travel from one coast to the other. Canals and steamboats simplified water travel and made shipping easier and less expensive. The **Erie Canal** (1825) connected the Great Lakes to the Hudson River. Other canals connected other major waterways, further facilitating transportation and the shipment of goods.

Transcontinental Railroad

In 1869, the **Union Pacific Railroad** completed the first section of a planned **transcontinental railroad**. This section went from Omaha, Nebraska to Sacramento, California. Ninety percent of the workers were Chinese, working in very dangerous conditions for very low pay. With the rise of the railroad, products were much more easily transported across the country. While this was positive overall for industry throughout the country, it was often damaging to family farmers, who found themselves paying high shipping costs for smaller supply orders while larger companies received major discounts.

Measures to Limit Immigration in the 19th Century

In 1870, the **Naturalization Act** put limits on US citizenship, allowing full citizenship only to whites and those of African descent. The **Chinese Exclusion Act of 1882** put limits on Chinese immigration. The **Immigration Act of 1882** taxed immigrants, charging 50 cents per person. These funds helped pay administrative costs for regulating immigration. **Ellis Island** opened in 1892 as a processing center for those arriving in New York. The year 1921 saw the **Emergency Quota Act** passed, also known as the **Johnson Quota Act**, which severely limited the number of immigrants allowed into the country.

Agriculture in the 19th Century

Technological Advances in Agricultural Changes

During the mid-1800s, irrigation techniques improved significantly. Advances occurred in cultivation and breeding, as well as fertilizer use and crop rotation. In the Great Plains, also known as the Great American Desert, the dense soil was finally cultivated with steel plows. In 1892, gasoline-powered tractors arrived, and they were widely used by 1900. Other advancements in agriculture's toolset included barbed wire fences, combines, silos, deep-water wells, and the cream separator.

Major Actions that Helped Improve Agriculture

Four major government actions that helped improve US agriculture in the 19th century are:

- The **Department of Agriculture** came into being in 1862, working for the interests of farmers and ranchers across the country.
- The **Morrill Land-Grant Acts** were a series of acts passed between 1862 and 1890, allowing land-grant colleges.
- In conjunction with land-grant colleges, the **Hatch Act of 1887** brought agriculture experiment stations into the picture, helping discover new farming techniques.
- In 1914, the **Smith-Lever Act** provided cooperative programs to help educate people about food, home economics, community development, and agriculture. Related agriculture extension programs helped farmers increase crop production to feed the rapidly growing nation.

Inventors from the 1800s

Major inventors from the 1800s and their inventions include:

- Alexander Graham Bell—the telephone
- Orville and Wilbur Wright—the airplane
- Richard Gatling—the machine gun
- Walter Hunt, Elias Howe, and Isaac Singer—the sewing machine
- Nikola Tesla—alternating current motor
- George Eastman—the Kodak camera
- Thomas Edison—the first commercially practical light bulbs, motion pictures, and the phonograph

- Samuel Morse—the telegraph
- Charles Goodyear—vulcanized rubber
- Cyrus McCormick—the reaper
- George Westinghouse—the transformer, the air brake

This was an active period for invention, with about 700,000 patents registered between 1860 and 1900.

Gilded Age

The time period from the end of the Civil War to the beginning of the First World War is often referred to as the **Gilded Age**, or the **Second Industrial Revolution**. The US was changing from an agricultural-based economy to an **industrial economy**, with rapid growth accompanying the shift. In addition, the country itself was expanding, spreading into the seemingly unlimited west.

This time period saw the beginning of banks, department stores, chain stores, and trusts—all familiar features of the modern-day landscape. Cities also grew rapidly, and large numbers of immigrants arrived in the country, swelling the urban ranks.

Review Video: The Gilded Age: An Overview
Visit mometrix.com/academy and enter code: 684770

Factors Leading to the Development of the Populist Party

A major **recession** struck the United States during the 1890s, with crop prices falling dramatically. **Drought** compounded the problems, leaving many American farmers in crippling debt. The **Farmers' Alliance** formed in 1875, drawing the rural poor into a single political entity.

Recession also affected the more industrial parts of the country. The **Knights of Labor**, formed in 1869 by **Uriah Stephens**, was able to unite workers into a union to protect their rights. Dissatisfied by views espoused by industrialists, the Farmers Alliance and the Knights of Labor, joined to form the **Populist Party**, also known as the People's Party, in 1892. Some of the elements of the party's platform included:

- National currency
- Graduated income tax
- Government ownership of railroads as well as telegraph and telephone systems
- Secret ballots for voting
- Immigration restriction
- Single-term limits for president and vice-president

The Populist Party was in favor of decreasing elitism and making the voice of the common man more easily heard in the political process.

Growth of the Labor Movement Through the Late 19th Century

One of the first large, well-organized strikes occurred in 1892. Called the **Homestead Strike**, it occurred when the Amalgamated Association of Iron and Steel Workers struck against the Carnegie Steel Company. Gunfire ensued, and Carnegie was able to eliminate the plant's union. In 1894, workers in the American Railway Union, led by Eugene Debs, initiated the **Pullman Strike** after the Pullman Palace Car Co. cut their wages by 28 percent. President Grover Cleveland called in troops to break up the strike on the grounds that it interfered with mail delivery. Mary Harris "Mother" Jones organized the **Children's Crusade** to protest child labor. A protest march proceeded to the home of President Theodore Roosevelt in 1903. Jones also worked with the United Mine Workers of America and helped found the **Industrial Workers of the World**.

Panic of 1893

Far from a US-centric event, the **Panic of 1893** was an economic crisis that affected most of the globe. As a response, President Grover Cleveland repealed the **Sherman Silver Purchase Act**, afraid it had caused the downturn rather than boosting the economy as intended. The Panic led to bankruptcies, with banks and railroads going under and factory unemployment rising as high as 25 percent. In the end, the **Republican Party** regained power due to the economic crisis.

Progressive Era

From the 1890s to the end of the First World War, **Progressives** set forth an ideology that drove many levels of society and politics. The Progressives were in favor of workers' rights and safety and wanted measures taken against waste and corruption. They felt science could help improve society and that the government could—and should—provide answers to a variety of social problems. Progressives came from a wide variety of backgrounds but were united in their desire to improve society.

Muckrakers and the Progressive Movement

"Muckrakers" was a term used to identify aggressive investigative journalists who exposed scandals, corruption, and many other wrongs in late 19th-century society. Among these intrepid writers were:

- **Ida Tarbell**—she exposed John D. Rockefeller's Standard Oil Trust.
- **Jacob Riis**—a photographer, he brought the living conditions of the poor in New York to the public's attention.
- **Lincoln Steffens**—he worked to expose political corruption in municipal government.
- **Upton Sinclair**—his book *The Jungle* led to reforms in the meat-packing industry.

Through the work of these journalists, many new policies came into being, including workmen's compensation, child labor laws, and trust-busting.

Dealings with Native Americans Through the End of the 19th Century

America's westward expansion led to conflict and violent confrontations with Native Americans such as the **Battle of Little Bighorn**. In 1876, the American government ordered all Native Americans to relocate to reservations. Lack of compliance led to the **Dawes Act** in 1887, which ordered assimilation rather than separation: Native Americans were offered American citizenship and a piece of their tribal land if they would accept the lot chosen by the government and live on it separately from the tribe. This act remained in effect until 1934. Reformers also forced Native American children to attend **boarding schools**, where they were not allowed to speak their native language and were immersed into a Euro-American culture and religion. Children were often abused in these schools and were indoctrinated to abandon their identity as Native Americans.

In 1890, the massacre at **Wounded Knee**, accompanied by Geronimo's surrender, led the Native Americans to work to preserve their culture rather than fight for their lands.

Review Video: Government Dealings with Native Americans Through 1900
Visit mometrix.com/academy and enter code: 635645

NATIVE AMERICANS IN WARTIME THROUGH THE BEGINNING OF THE 20TH CENTURY

The **Spanish-American War** (1898) saw a number of Native Americans serving with Teddy Roosevelt in the Rough Riders. Apache scouts accompanied General John J. Pershing to Mexico, hoping to find **Pancho Villa**. More than 17,000 Native Americans were drafted into service for **World War I**, though at the time, they were not considered legal citizens. In 1924, Native Americans were finally granted official citizenship by the **Indian Citizenship Act**.

After decades of relocation, forced assimilation, and genocide, the number of Native Americans in the US has greatly declined. Though many Native Americans have chosen—or have been forced—to assimilate, about 300 reservations exist today, with most of their inhabitants living in abject poverty.

Review Video: Wartime Role of Native Americans
Visit mometrix.com/academy and enter code: 419128

EVENTS LEADING UP TO THE SPANISH-AMERICAN WAR

Spain had controlled **Cuba** since the 15th century. Over the centuries, the Spanish had quashed a variety of revolts. In 1886, slavery ended in Cuba, and another revolt was rising.

In the meantime, the US had expressed interest in Cuba, offering Spain $130 million for the island in 1853, during Franklin Pierce's presidency. In 1898, the Cuban revolt was underway. In spite of various factions supporting the Cubans, the US President, William McKinley, refused to recognize the rebellion, preferring negotiation over involvement in war. Then, the *Maine*, a US battleship in Havana Harbor, was blown up, killing 266 crew members. The US declared war two months later, and the war ended with a **Spanish surrender** in less than four months.

American History 1899 to Present

INFLUENCE OF BIG STICK DIPLOMACY ON AMERICAN FOREIGN POLICY IN LATIN AMERICA

Theodore Roosevelt's famous quote, "Speak softly and carry a big stick," is supposedly of African origins, at least according to Roosevelt. He used this proverb to justify expanded involvement in foreign affairs during his tenure as President. The US military was deployed to protect American interests in **Latin America**. Roosevelt also worked to maintain an equal or greater influence in Latin America than those held by European interests. As a result, the US Navy grew larger, and the US generally became more involved in foreign affairs. Roosevelt felt that if any country was left vulnerable to control by Europe due to economic issues or political instability, the US had not only a right to intervene but was **obligated** to do so. This led to US involvement in Cuba, Nicaragua, Haiti, and the Dominican Republic over several decades leading into the First and Second World Wars.

IMPORTANCE OF THE PANAMA CANAL

Initial work began on the **Panama Canal** in 1881, though the idea had been discussed since the 1500s. The canal greatly reduces the length and time needed to sail from one ocean to the other by connecting the Atlantic to the Pacific through the Isthmus of Panama, which joins South America to North America. Before the canal was built, travelers had to sail around the entire perimeter of South America to reach the West Coast of the US. The French began the work after successfully completing the **Suez Canal**, which connected the Mediterranean Sea to the Red Sea. However, due to disease and high expense, the work moved slowly, and after eight years, the company went bankrupt, suspending work. The US purchased the holdings, and the first ship sailed through the canal in 1914. The Panama Canal was constructed as a lock-and-lake canal, with ships lifted on locks to travel from one lake to another over the rugged, mountainous terrain. In order to maintain control of the Canal Zone, the US assisted Panama in its battle for independence from **Colombia**.

Taft's Dollar Diplomacy vs. Roosevelt's Diplomatic Theories

During William Howard Taft's presidency, Taft instituted "**Dollar Diplomacy**." This approach was America's effort to influence Latin America and East Asia through economic rather than military means. Taft saw past efforts in these areas to be political and warlike, while his efforts focused on peaceful economic goals. His justification of the policy was to protect the **Panama Canal**, which was vital to US trade interests.

In spite of Taft's assurance that Dollar Diplomacy was a peaceful approach, many interventions proved violent. During Latin American revolts, such as those in **Nicaragua**, the US sent troops to settle the revolutions. Afterward, bankers moved in to help support the new leaders through loans. Dollar Diplomacy continued until 1913, when Woodrow Wilson was elected president.

Growth of Civil Rights for African Americans

Marcus Garvey founded the **Universal Negro Improvement Association and African Communities League (UNIA-ACL)**, which became a large and active organization focused on building black nationalism. In 1909, the **National Association for the Advancement of Colored People (NAACP)** came into being, working to defeat Jim Crow laws. The NAACP also helped prevent racial segregation from becoming federal law, fought against lynchings, helped black soldiers in WWI become officers, and helped defend the Scottsboro Boys, who were unjustly accused of rape.

Wilson's Approach to International Diplomacy

Turning away from Taft's "Dollar Diplomacy," Wilson instituted a foreign policy he referred to as "**moral diplomacy**." This approach still influences American foreign policy today.

Wilson felt that **representative government and democracy** in all countries would lead to worldwide stability. Democratic governments, he felt, would be less likely to threaten American interests. He also saw the US and Great Britain as the great role models in this area, as well as champions of world peace and self-government. Free trade and international commerce would allow the US to speak out regarding world events.

Main elements of Wilson's policies included:

- Maintaining a strong military
- Promoting democracy throughout the world
- Expanding international trade to boost the American economy

The Sixteenth, Seventeenth, Eighteenth, and Nineteenth Amendments

The early 20th century saw several amendments made to the US Constitution:

- The **Sixteenth Amendment** (1913) established a federal income tax.
- The **Seventeenth Amendment** (1913) allowed popular election of senators.
- The **Eighteenth Amendment** (1919) prohibited the sale, production, and transportation of alcohol. This amendment was later repealed by the Twenty-first Amendment.
- The **Nineteenth Amendment** (1920) gave women the right to vote.

These amendments largely grew out of the Progressive Era, as many citizens worked to improve American society.

Goals of the Anti-Defamation League

In 1913, the Anti-Defamation League was formed to prevent anti-Semitic behavior and practices. Its actions also worked to prevent all forms of racism and to prevent individuals from being discriminated against for any reason involving their race. They spoke against the Ku Klux Klan, as well as other racist or anti-Semitic organizations. This organization still works to fight discrimination against all minorities.

Role of the Federal Trade Commission in Eliminating Trusts

Muckrakers such as Ida Tarbell and Lincoln Steffens brought to light the damaging trend of trusts—huge corporations working to monopolize areas of commerce so they could control prices and distribution. The **Sherman Antitrust Act** and the **Clayton Antitrust Act** set out guidelines for competition among corporations and set out to eliminate these trusts. The **Federal Trade Commission** was formed in 1914 in order to enforce antitrust measures and ensure that companies were operated fairly and did not create controlling monopolies.

Major Events of World War I

World War I occurred from 1914 to 1918 and was fought largely in Europe. The rise in **nationalism** at the beginning of the 20th century helped contribute to the possibility of war. There was also some conflict between the **imperialist** (France, Britain, and the US) and the **non-imperialist** (Germany, Italy) nations. Many large nations were seeking economic expansion outside of their own borders, and the competition for foreign markets was intense. There was also a complex system of entangling alliances; many countries were involved in several different alliances at the same time. The spark for World War I, though, was the assassination of **Archduke Franz Ferdinand**, heir to the throne of Austria-Hungary, in April of 1914 by a Serbian nationalist. When Emperor Franz Joseph declared war on Serbia, it set off a chain reaction that involved virtually every nation in Europe. At the beginning of the conflict, Woodrow Wilson declared the US neutral. Eventually, however, the US joined the war. Major events influencing US involvement included:

- **Sinking of the *Lusitania***—the British passenger liner RMS *Lusitania* was sunk by a German U-boat in 1915. Among the 1,000 civilian victims were over 100 American citizens. Outraged by this act, many Americans began to push for US involvement in the war, using the *Lusitania* as a rallying cry.
- **German U-boat aggression**—Wilson continued to keep the US out of the war, using as his 1916 reelection slogan, "He kept us out of war." While he continued to work toward an end of the war, German U-boats began to indiscriminately attack American and Canadian merchant ships carrying supplies to Germany's enemies in Europe.
- **Zimmerman Telegram** —the final event that brought the US into World War I was the interception of the Zimmerman Telegram (also known as the Zimmerman Note) on January 17th, 1917. In this telegram, Germany proposed forming an alliance with Mexico if the US entered the war.

Efforts in the US During World War I Supporting the War Effort

American **railroads** came under government control in December 1917. The widespread system was consolidated into a single system, with each region assigned a director. This greatly increased the efficiency of the railroad system, allowing the railroads to supply both domestic and military needs. Control returned to private ownership in 1920. In 1918, **telegraph, telephone, and cable services** also came under Federal control, to be returned to private management the next year. The **American Red Cross** supported the war effort by knitting clothes for Army and Navy troops. They also helped supply hospital and refugee clothing and surgical dressings. Over 8 million people participated in this effort. To generate wartime funds, the US government sold **Liberty Bonds**. In four issues, they sold nearly $25 billion—more than one-fifth of Americans purchased them. After the war, a fifth bond drive was held but sold "**Victory Liberty Bonds**."

Review Video: WWI Overview
Visit mometrix.com/academy and enter code: 659767

Influence of Wilson's Fourteen Points on Final Peace Treaties

President Woodrow Wilson proposed **Fourteen Points** as the basis for a peace settlement to end the war. Presented to the US Congress in January 1918, the Fourteen Points included:

- Five points outlining **general ideals**
- Eight points to resolve **immediate problems** of political and territorial nature
- One point proposing an **organization of nations** (the League of Nations) with the intent of maintaining world peace

In November of that same year, Germany agreed to an **armistice**, assuming the final treaty would be based on the Fourteen Points. However, during the peace conference in Paris 1919, there was much disagreement, leading to a final agreement that punished Germany and the other Central Powers much more than originally intended. Henry Cabot Lodge, who had become the Foreign Relations Committee chairman in 1918, wanted an unconditional surrender from Germany and was concerned about the article in the **Treaty of Versailles** that gave the League of Nations power to declare war without a vote from the US Congress. A **League of Nations** was included in the Treaty of Versailles at Wilson's insistence. The Senate rejected the Treaty of Versailles, and in the end, Wilson refused to concede to Lodge's demands. As a result, the US did not join the League of Nations.

Origins of the Red Scare

World War I created many jobs, but after the war ended, these jobs disappeared, leaving many unemployed. In the wake of these employment changes, the **International Workers of the World** and the **Socialist Party**, headed by Eugene Debs, became more and more visible. Workers initiated strikes in an attempt to regain the favorable working conditions that had been put into place before the war. Unfortunately, many of these strikes became violent, and the actions were blamed on "Reds," or Communists, for trying to spread their views into America. With the recent Bolshevik Revolution in Russia, many Americans feared a similar revolution might occur in the US. The **Red Scare** ensued, with many individuals jailed for supposedly holding communist, anarchist, or socialist beliefs.

Major Changes and Events that Took Place in America During the 1920s

The post-war 1920s saw many Americans moving from the farm to the city, with growing prosperity in the US. The **Roaring Twenties**, or the **Jazz Age**, was driven largely by growth in the automobile and entertainment industries. Individuals like Charles Lindbergh, the first aviator to make a solo flight across the Atlantic Ocean, added to the American admiration of individual accomplishment. Telephone lines, distribution of electricity, highways, the radio, and other inventions brought great changes to everyday life.

Review Video: 1920's
Visit mometrix.com/academy and enter code: 124996

Prohibition

The Eighteenth Amendment was ratified by most states in 1919, making the manufacture, sale, transportation, importation, and exportation of alcohol illegal; however, this change was not enforced with much success. Instead of curbing the production and consumption of alcohol, Prohibition led to the creation of a large, illegal alcohol market dominated by organized crime. Criminal organizations, like the Mafia crime syndicate, grew massively in power and influence during the 1920s and 1930s by cornering the market on the production, distribution, and sale of alcohol. Americans continued to drink alcohol in speakeasies—hidden, illegal drinking establishments. The huge illegal market for alcohol contributed to increased crime and unregulated, sometimes dangerous, alcohol.

Major Cultural Movements of the 1920s Influenced by African Americans

The **Harlem Renaissance** saw a number of African-American artists settling in Harlem in New York. This community produced a number of well-known artists and writers, including Langston Hughes, Nella Larsen, Zora Neale Hurston, Claude McKay, Countee Cullen, and Jean Toomer. The growth of jazz, also largely driven by African Americans, defined the **Jazz Age**. Its unconventional, improvisational style matched the growing sense of optimism and exploration of the decade. Originating as an offshoot of the blues, jazz began in New Orleans. Some significant jazz musicians were Duke Ellington, Louis Armstrong, and Jelly Roll Morton. **Big Band** and **Swing Jazz** also developed in the 1920s. Well-known musicians of this movement included Bing Crosby, Frank Sinatra, Count Basie, Benny Goodman, Billie Holiday, Ella Fitzgerald, and The Dorsey Brothers.

American Civil Liberties Union

The American Civil Liberties Union (**ACLU**), founded in 1920, grew from the American Union Against Militarism. The ACLU helped conscientious objectors avoid going to war during WWI, and also helped those being prosecuted under the **Espionage Act** (1917) and the **Sedition Act** (1918), many of whom were immigrants. Their major goals were to protect immigrants and other citizens who were threatened with prosecution for their political beliefs, and to support labor unions, which were also under threat by the government during the Red Scare.

Womens' Suffrage

The Nineteenth Amendment gave **women the right to vote**. This amendment was proposed on June 4, 1919, and was ratified on August 18, 1920. An amendment to give women the right to vote was first introduced in Congress in 1878, but it failed to pass. For the next four decades, the amendment was reintroduced in every session of Congress but was defeated each time. The involvement of women in the war effort during World War I spawned increased support for women's suffrage. Finally, in 1918, the House of Representatives approved the amendment to grant women suffrage, but the Senate defeated it. In 1919, the Senate also passed the amendment and sent it to the states for approval, where it was ratified in 1920.

Provisions and Importance of the National Origins Act of 1924

The National Origins Act (Johnson-Reed Act) placed limitations on **immigration**. The number of immigrants allowed into the US was based on the population of each nationality of immigrants who were living in the country in 1890. Only two percent of each nationality's 1890 population numbers were allowed to immigrate. This led to great disparities between immigrants from various nations, and Asian immigration was not allowed at all. Some of the impetus behind the Johnson-Reed Act came as a result of paranoia following the **Russian Revolution**. Fear of communist influences in the US led to a general fear of immigrants.

Ku Klux Klan

In 1866, Confederate Army veterans came together to fight against Reconstruction in the South, forming a group called the **Ku Klux Klan (KKK)**. With white supremacist beliefs, including anti-Semitism, nativism, anti-Catholicism, and overt racism, this organization relied heavily on violence to get its message across. In 1915, they grew again in power, using a film called *The Birth of a Nation*, by D.W. Griffith, to spread their ideas. In the 1920s, the reach of the KKK spread far into the north and midwest, and members controlled a number of state governments. Its membership and power began to decline during the Great Depression but experienced a resurgence later.

The Great Depression

The **Great Depression** was the largest economic downturn in the history of the United States. It began in 1929 with the stock market crash and ended around 1939. The Great Depression grew out of several factors that had developed over the previous years, including:

- Growing economic disparity between the rich and middle classes, with the rich amassing wealth much more quickly than the lower classes
- Disparity in economic distribution in industries
- Growing use of credit, leading to an inflated demand for some goods
- Government support of new industries rather than agriculture
- Risky stock market investments, leading to the stock market crash

Additional factors contributing to the Depression also included the **Labor Day Hurricane** in the Florida Keys (1935) and the **Great Hurricane of 1938** in New England, along with the **Dust Bowl** in the Great Plains, which destroyed crops and resulted in the displacement of as many as 2.5 million people.

Review Video: Causes of the Great Depression
Visit mometrix.com/academy and enter code: 635912

The Dust Bowl

The Dust Bowl (1930-1941) was a period of American history characterized by a high incidence of dust storms in the Great Plains region. The instability of the world agriculture market during World War I led to overproduction in the 1920s. Even lands previously considered unsuitable for agricultural use were leveled and developed. This excessive activity devastated the Great Plains, eliminating the natural vegetation that could have prevented the massive soil movement that occurred during the drought and strong winds of the 1930s, and resulted in widespread crop failure. In turn, the Dust Bowl led to millions of people being displaced from their homes and hundreds of thousands migrating to California in search of work and better living conditions. On their journeys, however, these migrants faced poor conditions, starvation, and dehydration. Even when they arrived in California, many of them struggled to find work. The work that was available was often hard labor, like picking cotton. Migrants also faced hostility and even phyisical violence from locals. They were often forced to live in roadside camps, which were sometimes the target of arson.

Franklin D. Roosevelt's Election and New Deal

Franklin D. Roosevelt was elected president in 1932 with his promise of a "**New Deal**" for Americans. His goals were to provide government work programs to provide jobs, wages, and relief to numerous workers throughout the beleaguered US. Congress gave Roosevelt almost free rein to produce relief legislation. The goals of this legislation were:

- **Relief**—creating jobs for the high numbers of unemployed
- **Recovery**—stimulating the economy through the National Recovery Administration
- **Reform**—passing legislation to prevent future, similar economic crashes

The Roosevelt Administration also passed legislation regarding ecological issues, including the Soil Conservation Service, aimed at preventing another Dust Bowl.

Roosevelt's Alphabet Organizations

So-called "alphabet organizations" set up during Roosevelt's administration included:

- **Civilian Conservation Corps** (CCC)—provided jobs in the forestry service
- **Agricultural Adjustment Administration** (AAA)—increased agricultural income by adjusting both production and prices
- **Tennessee Valley Authority** (TVA)—organized projects to build dams in the Tennessee River for flood control and production of electricity, resulting in increased productivity for industries in the area, and easier navigation of the Tennessee River
- **Public Works Administration** (PWA) and Civil Works Administration (CWA)—provided a multitude of jobs, initiating over 34,000 projects
- **Works Progress Administration** (WPA)—helped unemployed persons to secure employment on government work projects or elsewhere

Actions Taken During the Roosevelt Administration to Prevent Future Crashes

The Roosevelt administration passed several laws and established several institutions to initiate the "reform" portion of the New Deal, including:

- **Glass-Steagall Act**—separated investment from commercial banking
- **Securities Exchange Commission (SEC)**—helped regulate Wall Street investment practices, making them less dangerous to the overall economy
- **Wagner Act**—provided worker and union rights to improve relations between employees and employers
- **Social Security Act of 1935**—provided pensions as well as unemployment insurance

Other actions focused on insuring bank deposits and adjusting the value of American currency. Most of these regulatory agencies and government policies and programs still exist today.

Major Regulations Regarding Labor During the Great Depression

Three major regulations regarding labor that were passed after the Great Depression are:

- **Davis-Bacon Act** (1931)—provided fair compensation for contractors and subcontractors.
- The **Wagner Act** (1935)—also known as the National Labor Relations Act, it established that unions were legal, protected members of unions, and required collective bargaining. This act was later amended by the Taft-Hartley Act of 1947 and the Landrum-Griffin Act of 1959, which further clarified certain elements.
- **Walsh-Healey Act** (1936)—established a minimum wage, child labor laws, safety standards, and overtime pay.

World War II

America's Introduction to WWII

After the First World War, the US became obsessed with isolating itself from foreign conflicts. The **Nye Committee** studied the war and determined that it had been fought for financial reasons and could have been avoided. Isolationist parties achieved some popularity during this period, including the **America First Committee**, led by Charles Lindbergh, and **SOS** (Stop Organized Slaughter). The **Neutrality Laws** of 1935-7 declared that the US could not sell weapons to another country in a time of war and that US citizens could not travel on the ships of a nation at war. In 1937, FDR delivered the **Quarantine Speech**, in which he asserted that the Nazi "disease" must be contained. Finally, after conflict in Europe had escalated considerably, FDR declared that the US needed to help Britain and be an "arsenal of democracy in the world." The **Neutrality Act of 1940** made it legal for the US to sell weapons on a cash and carry basis. In August of 1941, FDR and Churchill drew up the **Atlantic Charter**, which vowed to destroy Nazism, protect the right of self-determination, and create a World Peace Organization.

Buildup to the Attack on Pearl Harbor

A number of events had created a stormy relationship between the US and Japan long before the invasion of Pearl Harbor, but the conflict reached a boiling point after President Roosevelt froze all Japanese assets in the US and cut Japan off from US oil and steel. America also had a cordial relationship at this time with Japan's longtime rival, China. The Japanese launched surprise attacks both on the American naval base at **Pearl Harbor** and on the **Philippines**, where they hoped to secure some oil.

US Involvement in WWII Concerning Europe and Africa

After the Japanese attack on Pearl Harbor in 1941, the US declared **war** on Japan, after which Germany declared war on the US. Before going after Japan, however, the US first attacked Germany; this was done because the US underestimated Japan industrially and militarily, and because the US feared Britain was on the verge of defeat. **Operation Overlord**, the Allied invasion of the European continent at Normandy, was led in part by General **Dwight D. Eisenhower**. The American generals Omar Bradley and George Patton took part in the **Allied Operation Torch**, aimed at taking back North Africa. At the **Battle of the Bulge**, in Belgium, the Germans tried to break the Allied lines, but were unsuccessful, in part because of the heroism of American soldiers.

US Involvement in WWII Concerning Asia and the Pacific

The US strategy for controlling the Pacific was known as "island hopping." In the **Coral Sea Battle of 1942**, Americans stopped the Japanese from taking Australia and New Guinea. In the same year, the **Doolittle raids** of Japanese naval bases boosted American morale. In the **Battle of Midway** (1942), the US sunk four Japanese aircraft carriers. In the **Battle of Leyte Gulf**, General Douglas MacArthur took back the Philippines and also took control of Iwo Jima and Okinawa. During this period, a team of American scientists led by Robert Oppenheimer was developing the **atomic bomb** in Los Alamos, New Mexico. Japan was warned several times by President Truman that the bomb would be used if they did not surrender. Surely enough, Americans dropped atomic bombs on **Hiroshima** on August 6, 1945, and on **Nagasaki** three days later. Japanese leaders surrendered aboard the USS Missouri on August 15, 1945.

The Holocaust is the name given to the systematic killing of Jews, Gypsies, homosexuals, and others by the Nazis. **Anti-Semitism** had existed in Europe for a long time, but the Nazis gave it renewed emphasis and, after making numerous false claims about Jews, began persecuting them upon Hitler's rise to power in 1933. Jews were disenfranchised, forced into ghettos, had their property taken, and were finally sent to work and be killed in **concentration camps**. Approximately 6 million Jews were killed during the **Holocaust**. As the situation for the Germans became more dire in the Second World War, Hitler sought to implement what he called the "final solution," in which hundreds of thousands were killed just before the fall of Nazi Germany.

Interventionist and Isolationist Approaches in World War II

When war broke out in Europe in 1939, President Roosevelt stated that the US would remain **neutral**. However, his overall approach was considered "**interventionist**," as he was willing to provide aid to the Allies without actually entering the conflict. Thus, the US supplied a wide variety of war materials to the Allied nations in the early years of the war.

Isolationists believed the US should not provide any aid to the Allies, including supplies. They felt Roosevelt, by assisting the Allies, was leading the US into a war for which it was not prepared. Led by Charles Lindbergh, the Isolationists believed that any involvement in the European conflict endangered the US by weakening its national defense.

Sequence of Events that Led the US to Declare War and Enter World War II

In 1937, Japan invaded China, prompting the US to eventually halt exports to Japan. Roosevelt also did not allow Japanese interests to withdraw money held in US banks. In 1941, **General Tojo** rose to power as the Japanese prime minister. Recognizing America's ability to bring a halt to Japan's expansion, he authorized the bombing of **Pearl Harbor** on December 7. The US responded by declaring war on Japan. Partially because of the **Tripartite Pact** among the Axis Powers, Germany and Italy then declared war on the US, later followed by Bulgaria, Hungary, and other Axis nations.

Review Video: World War II Overview
Visit mometrix.com/academy and enter code: 759402

Occurrences of World War II that Led to the Surrender of Germany

In 1941, **Hitler** violated the non-aggression pact he had signed with Stalin two years earlier by invading the USSR. **Stalin** then joined the **Allies**. Stalin, Roosevelt, and Winston Churchill planned to defeat Germany first, then Japan, bringing the war to an end.

In 1942-1943, the Allies drove **Axis** forces out of Africa. In addition, the Germans were soundly defeated at Stalingrad.

The **Italian Campaign** involved Allied operations in Italy between July 1943 and May 1945, including Italy's liberation. On June 6, 1944, known as **D-Day**, the Allies invaded France at Normandy. Soviet troops moved on the eastern front at the same time, driving German forces back. By April 25, 1945, Berlin was surrounded by Soviet troops. On May 7, Germany surrendered.

Major Events of World War II that Led to the Surrender of Japan

War continued with **Japan** after Germany's surrender. Japanese forces had taken a large portion of Southeast Asia and the Western Pacific, all the way to the Aleutian Islands in Alaska. **General Doolittle** bombed several Japanese cities while American troops scored a victory at Midway. Additional fighting in the Battle of the Coral Sea further weakened Japan's position. As a final blow, the US dropped two **atomic bombs** on Japan, one on Hiroshima and the other on Nagasaki. This was the first time atomic bombs had been used in warfare, and the devastation was horrific and demoralizing. Japan surrendered on September 2, 1945, which became **V-J Day** in the US.

The 442nd Regimental Combat Team, Tuskegee Airmen, and Navajo Code Talkers

The 442nd Regimental Combat Team consisted of Japanese-Americans fighting in Europe for the US. The most highly decorated unit per member in US history, they suffered a 93% casualty rate during the war. The **Tuskegee Airmen** were African American aviators, the first black Americans allowed to fly for the military. In spite of being ineligible to become official navy pilots, they flew over 15,000 missions and were highly decorated. The **Navajo Code Talkers** were native Navajo who used their traditional language to transmit information among Allied forces. Because Navajo is a highly-complex and unwritten language and not simply a code, the Axis powers were never able to translate it. The use of Navajo Code Talkers to transmit information was instrumental in the taking of Iwo Jima and other major victories of the war.

Circumstances and Opportunities for Women During World War II

Women served widely in the military during WWII, working in numerous positions, including the **Flight Nurses Corps**. Women also moved into the workforce while men were overseas, leading to over 19 million women in the US workforce by 1944. **Rosie the Riveter** stood as a symbol of these women and a means of recruiting others to take needed positions. Women, as well as their families left behind during wartime, also grew **Victory Gardens** to help provide food.

Japanese-American Internment During World War II

Following the attack on Pearl Harbor, the American government began to suspect that people of Japanese ancestry in America may be operating as spies for Japan, though there was little evidence for this. Just a couple of months after the attack, President Franklin D. Roosevelt signed Executive Order 9066, which allowed the government to declare Military Exclusion Zones for the purpose of national security. This made it legal for the military to remove people or other perceived threats from these exclusion zones. As a result, over 100,000 people of Japanese ancestry were removed from their homes in these areas and placed into internment camps. These camps were hastily built and offered poor living conditions. Children interned in these camps did not have access to a full education, and many Japanese-Americans lost their businesses and homes as a result of their internment.

In **Korematsu v. US** (1944), the Supreme Court ruled that the internment camps were legal, but in **ex parte Endo** (1944), the Court adjusted its decision to state that the US could only intern those whose disloyalty could be proven. Japanese internment ended in 1945, but the effects of internment on Japanese-Americans endured.

Importance of the Atomic Bomb During World War II

The atomic bomb, developed during WWII, was the most powerful bomb ever invented. A single bomb, carried by a single plane, held enough power to destroy an entire city. This devastating effect was demonstrated with the bombing of **Hiroshima** and **Nagasaki** in 1945 in what later became a controversial move, but ended the war. The bombings resulted in as many as 150,000 immediate deaths and many more as time passed after the bombings, mostly due to **radiation poisoning**.

Whatever the arguments against the use of "The Bomb," the post-WWII era saw many countries develop similar weapons to match the newly expanded military power of the US. The impact of those developments and use of nuclear weapons continues to haunt international relations today.

Importance of the Yalta Conference and the Potsdam Conference

In February 1945, Joseph Stalin, Franklin D. Roosevelt, and Winston Churchill met in Yalta to discuss the post-war treatment of the **Axis nations**, particularly Germany. Though Germany had not yet surrendered, its defeat was imminent. After Germany's official surrender, Joseph Stalin,

Harry Truman (Roosevelt's successor), and Clement Attlee (replacing Churchill partway through the conference) met to formalize those plans. This meeting was called the **Potsdam Conference**. Basic provisions of these agreements included:

- Dividing Germany and Berlin into four zones of occupation
- Demilitarization of Germany
- Poland remaining under Soviet control
- Outlawing the Nazi Party
- Trials for Nazi leaders
- Relocation of numerous German citizens
- The USSR joining the United Nations, established in 1945
- Establishment of the United Nations Security Council, consisting of the US, the UK, the USSR, China, and France

Agreements Made with Post-War Japan

General Douglas MacArthur led the American **military occupation of Japan** after the country surrendered. The goals of the US occupation included removing Japan's military and making the country a democracy. A 1947 constitution removed power from the emperor and gave it to the people, as well as granting voting rights to women. Japan was no longer allowed to declare war, and a group of 28 government officials were tried for war crimes. In 1951, the US finally signed a peace treaty with Japan. This treaty allowed Japan to rearm itself for purposes of self-defense but stripped the country of the empire it had built overseas.

US Treatment of Immigrants During and After World War II

In 1940, the US passed the **Alien Registration Act**, which required all aliens older than fourteen to be fingerprinted and registered. They were also required to report changes of address within five days.

Tension between whites and Japanese immigrants in **California**, which had been building since the beginning of the century, came to a head with the bombing of **Pearl Harbor** in 1941. Believing that even those Japanese living in the US were likely to be loyal to their native country, the president ordered numerous Japanese to be arrested on suspicion of subversive action and isolated in exclusion zones known as **War Relocation Camps**. Approximately 120,000 Japanese-Americans, two-thirds of them US citizens, were sent to these camps during the war.

General State of the US After World War II

Following WWII, the US became the strongest political power in the world, becoming a major player in world affairs and foreign policies. The US determined to stop the spread of **communism**, having named itself the "**arsenal of democracy**" during the war. In addition, America emerged with a greater sense of itself as a single, integrated nation, with many regional and economic differences diminished. The government worked for greater equality, and the growth of communications increased contact among different areas of the country. Both the aftermath of the Great Depression and the necessities of WWII had given the government greater **control** over various institutions as well as the economy. This also meant that the American government took on greater responsibility for the well-being of its citizens, both in the domestic arena, such as providing basic needs, and in protecting them from foreign threats. This increased role of providing basic necessities for all Americans has been criticized by some as "**the welfare state.**"

Fear of Communism Following World War II

After World War II, America became greatly concerned with the spread of communism, which was being propagated mainly by the Soviet Union and the communist party in China. A series of policies in America, Western Europe, and the Soviet Union brought the anti-communist and communist groups ever closer to open conflict. As these tensions grew in the international community, Americans became increasingly paranoid about the spread of **Communism**. There were numerous investigations aimed at weeding Communist spies out of the government, and two people, Julius and Ethel Rosenberg, were executed for spying. The leader of much of this was Senator **Joseph McCarthy**, who was famous for promoting and prolonging the "**Red Scare**" as the often-termed witch-hunt for communists in the government was known (Soviet communications released after the fall of the Soviet Union confirmed the vast majority of his accusations). The tide of anti-communism extended into a general disapproval of organized labor. The **Taft-Hartley Act** restricted the ability of labor unions markedly. In order to survive, the nation's two largest labor unions combined, forming the **AFL-CIO**.

US Policy Toward Immigrants After World War II

Prior to WWII, the US had been limiting **immigration** for several decades. After WWII, policy shifted slightly to accommodate political refugees from Europe and elsewhere. So many people were displaced by the war that in 1946, the UN formed the **International Refugee Organization** to deal with the problem. In 1948, the US Congress passed the **Displaced Persons Act**, which allowed over 400,000 European refugees to enter the US, most of them concentration camp survivors and refugees from Eastern Europe.

In 1952, the **United States Escapee Program (USEP)** increased the quotas, allowing refugees from communist Europe to enter the US, as did the **Refugee Relief Act**, passed in 1953. At the same time, however, the **Internal Security Act of 1950** allowed deportation of declared communists, and Asians were subjected to a quota based on race, rather than country of origin. Later changes included:

- **Migration and Refugee Assistance Act** (1962)—provided aid for refugees in need
- **Immigration and Nationality Act** (1965)—ended quotas based on nation of origin
- **Immigration Reform and Control Act** (1986)—prohibited the hiring of illegal immigrants but also granted amnesty to about three million illegals already in the country

Accomplishments of Harry S. Truman

Harry S. Truman took over the presidency from Franklin D. Roosevelt near the end of WWII. He made the final decision to drop atomic bombs on Japan and played a major role in the final decisions regarding the treatment of post-war Germany. On the domestic front, Truman initiated a 21-point plan known as the **Fair Deal**. This plan expanded Social Security, provided public housing, and made the Fair Employment Practice Committee permanent. Truman helped support Greece and Turkey (which were under threat from the USSR), supported South Korea against communist North Korea, and helped with recovery in Western Europe. He also participated in the formation of **NATO**, the North Atlantic Treaty Organization.

Events and Importance of the Korean War

The Korean War began in 1950 and ended in 1953. For the first time in history, a world organization—the **United Nations**—played a military role in a war. North Korea sent communist troops into South Korea, seeking to bring the entire country under communist control. The UN sent out a call to member nations, asking them to support South Korea. Truman sent troops, as did many other UN member nations. The war ended three years later with a **truce** rather than a peace treaty, and Korea remains divided at the **38th parallel north**, with communist rule remaining in the North and a democratic government ruling the South.

Effects of US Cold War Foreign Policy Acts on the International Relationships

The following are US Cold War foreign policy acts and how they affected international relationships, especially between the US and the Soviet Union:

- **Marshall Plan**—this sent aid to war-torn Europe after WWII, largely focusing on preventing the spread of communism.
- **Containment Policy**—proposed by George F. Kennan, the containment policy focused on containing the spread of Soviet communism.
- **Truman Doctrine**—Harry S. Truman stated that the US would provide both economic and military support to any country threatened by Soviet takeover.
- **National Security Act**—passed in 1947, this act reorganized the government's military departments into the Department of Defense and created the Central Intelligence Agency and the National Security Council.

The combination of these acts led to the **Cold War**, with Soviet communists attempting to spread their influence and the US and other countries trying to contain or stop this spread.

Accomplishments of Dwight D. Eisenhower

Eisenhower carried out a middle-of-the-road foreign policy and brought the US several steps forward in equal rights. He worked to minimize tensions during the Cold War and negotiated a peace treaty with Russia after the death of Stalin. He enforced desegregation by sending troops to Little Rock Central High School in Arkansas, as well as ordering the desegregation of the military. Organizations formed during his administration included the Department of Health, Education, and Welfare, and the National Aeronautics and Space Administration (NASA).

Effect of the Arms Race on Post WWII International Relations

After World War II, major nations, particularly the US and USSR, rushed to develop highly advanced weapons systems such as the **atomic bomb** and later the **hydrogen bomb**. These countries seemed determined to outpace each other with the development of numerous, deadly weapons. These weapons were expensive and extremely dangerous, and it is possible that the war between US and Soviet interests remained "cold" due to the fear that one side or the other would use these powerful weapons.

Technological Advances that Occurred Throughout the 1900s

Numerous technological advances throughout the 1900s led to more effective treatment of diseases, more efficient communication and transportation, and new means of generating power. Advances in **medicine** increased the human lifespan in developed countries, and near-instantaneous **communication** opened up a myriad of possibilities. Some of these advances include:

- Discovery of penicillin (1928)
- Supersonic air travel (1947)
- Nuclear power plants (1951)
- Orbital satellite leading to manned space flight (Sputnik, 1957)
- First man on the moon (1969)

NATO, Warsaw Pact, and the Berlin Wall

NATO, the **North Atlantic Treaty Organization**, came into being in 1949. It essentially amounted to an agreement among the US and Western European countries that an attack on any one of these countries was to be considered an attack against the entire group. Under the influence of the Soviet Union, the Eastern European countries of the USSR, Bulgaria, East Germany, Poland, Romania, Albania, Hungary, and Czechoslovakia responded with the **Warsaw Pact**, which created a similar agreement among those nations. In 1961, a wall was built to separate communist East Berlin from democratic West Berlin. This was a literal representation of the "**Iron Curtain**" that separated the democratic and communist countries throughout the world.

Presidency of John F. Kennedy

Although his term was cut short by his assassination, **JFK** instituted economic programs that led to a period of continuous expansion in the US unmatched since before WWII. He formed the Alliance for Progress and the Peace Corps, organizations intended to help developing nations. He also oversaw the passage of new civil rights legislation and drafted plans to attack poverty and its causes, along with support of the arts. Kennedy's presidency ended when he was assassinated by **Lee Harvey Oswald** in 1963.

Events of the Cuban Missile Crisis

The Cuban Missile Crisis occurred in 1962, during John F. Kennedy's presidency. Russian Premier **Nikita Khrushchev** decided to place nuclear missiles in **Cuba** to protect the island from invasion by the US. An American U-2 plane flying over the island photographed the missile bases as they were being built. Tensions rose, with the US concerned about nuclear missiles so close to its shores, and the USSR concerned about American missiles that had been placed in **Turkey**. Eventually, the missile sites were removed, and a US naval blockade turned back Soviet ships carrying missiles to Cuba. During negotiations, the US agreed to remove their missiles from Turkey and agreed to sell surplus wheat to the USSR. A telephone hotline between Moscow and Washington was set up to allow instant communication between the two heads of state to prevent similar incidents in the future.

Accomplishments of the Lyndon B. Johnson Presidency

Kennedy's vice president, **Lyndon Johnson**, assumed the presidency after Kennedy's **assassination**. He supported civil rights bills, tax cuts, and other wide-reaching legislation that Kennedy had also supported. Johnson saw America as a "**Great Society**," and enacted legislation to fight disease and poverty, renew urban areas, and support education and environmental conservation. Medicare and Medicaid were instituted under his administration. He continued Kennedy's support of space exploration, and he is also known, although less positively, for his handling of the **Vietnam War**.

Factors that Led to the Growth of the Civil Rights Movement

In the 1950s, post-war America was experiencing a rapid growth in prosperity; however, African Americans found themselves left behind. Racial segregation and discrimination were still legalized at this time and disproportionately affected black Americans and other minority groups. The civil rights movement arose to abolish legalized discrimination and provide equality for all Americans.

While there were many different ideologies that made up the civil rights movement, the movement is largely characterized by peaceful protest and civil disobedience.

- **Rosa Parks**—often called the "mother of the Civil Rights Movement," her refusal to give up her seat on the bus to a white man served as a seed from which the movement grew.
- **Martin Luther King, Jr.**—the best-known leader of the movement, King drew on Gandhi's beliefs and encouraged non-violent opposition. He led a march on Washington in 1963, received the Nobel Peace Prize in 1964, and was assassinated in 1968.
- **Malcolm X**—espousing less peaceful means of change, Malcolm X became a Black Muslim and supported black nationalism.

Policies and Legislation Enacted Expanding Minority Rights

Several major acts have been passed, particularly since WWII, to protect the rights of minorities in America. These include:

- Civil Rights Act (1964)
- Voting Rights Act (1965)
- Age Discrimination Act (1967)
- Americans with Disabilities Act (1990)

Other important movements for civil rights included a prisoner's rights movement, movements for immigrant rights, and the women's rights movement. The National Organization for Women (NOW) was established in 1966 and worked to pass the Equal Rights Amendment. The amendment was passed, but not enough states ratified it for it to become part of the US Constitution.

Impact of Stokely Carmichael, Adam Clayton Powell, and Jesse Jackson

- **Stokely Carmichael**—Carmichael originated the term "Black Power" and served as head of the Student Nonviolent Coordinating Committee. He believed in black pride and black culture and felt separate political and social institutions should be developed for blacks.
- **Adam Clayton Powell**—chairman of the Coordinating Committee for Employment, he led rent strikes and other actions, as well as a bus boycott, to increase the hiring of blacks.
- **Jesse Jackson**—Jackson was selected to head the Chicago Operation Breadbasket in 1966, and went on to organize boycotts and other actions. He also had an unsuccessful run for president.

Events of the Civil Rights Movement

Major events of the Civil Rights Movement include:

- **Montgomery Bus Boycott**—in 1955, Rosa Parks refused to give her seat on the bus to a white man. As a result, she was tried and convicted of disorderly conduct and of violating local ordinances. A 381-day bus boycott ensued, protesting segregation on public buses.
- **Desegregation of Little Rock**—in 1957, after the Supreme Court decision on Brown v. Board of Education, which declared "separate but equal" unconstitutional, the Arkansas school board voted to desegregate their schools. Even though Arkansas was considered progressive, its governor brought in the Arkansas National Guard to prevent nine black students from entering Central High School in Little Rock. President Eisenhower responded by federalizing the National Guard and ordering them to stand down.

- **Birmingham Campaign**—protestors organized a variety of actions such as sit-ins and an organized march to launch a voting campaign. When the City of Birmingham declared the protests illegal, the protestors, including Martin Luther King, Jr., persisted and were arrested and jailed.
- **March on Washington**—on August 28, 1963, more than 200,000 people marched on Washington, D.C. to advocate for civil and economic rights for African Americans. Dr. Martin Luther King Jr., positioned near the Lincoln Memorial, gave his famous "I Have a Dream" speech. This march was heavily influential in passing the Civil Rights Act of 1964.

Pieces of Legislation Passed as a Result of the Civil Rights Movement

Other pieces of legislation passed as a result of the Civil Rights movement include:

- **Brown v. Board of Education** (1954)—the Supreme Court declared that "separate but equal" accommodations and services were unconstitutional.
- **Civil Rights Act of 1964**—this declared discrimination illegal in employment, education, or public accommodation.
- **Voting Rights Act of 1965**—this act ended various activities practiced, mostly in the South, to bar blacks from exercising their voting rights. These included poll taxes and literacy tests.
- **Fair Housing Act of 1968**—this act prohibited discrimination in the sale, purchase, and rental of housing.

Other pieces of legislation that expanded minority rights include the Age Discrimination Act (1967) and the Americans with Disabilities Act (1990). Other important movements for civil rights included prisoners' rights movements, movements for immigrant rights, and the women's rights movement. The National Organization for Women (NOW) was established in 1966 and worked to pass the Equal Rights Amendment. The amendment was passed, but not enough states ratified it for it to become part of the US Constitution.

Events of the Richard Nixon Presidency

Richard Nixon is best known for the **Watergate scandal** during his presidency, but other important events marked his tenure as president, including:

- End of the Vietnam War
- Improved diplomatic relations between the US and China, and the US and the USSR
- National Environmental Policy Act passed, providing for environmental protection
- Compulsory draft ended
- Supreme Court legalized abortion in Roe v. Wade (subsequently overturned in 2022)
- Watergate

The Watergate scandal of 1972 ended Nixon's presidency. Rather than face impeachment and removal from office, he **resigned** in 1974.

US Perspective on the Progression of the Vietnam War

After World War II, the US pledged, as part of its foreign policy, to come to the assistance of any country threatened by **communism**. When Vietnam was divided into a communist North and democratic South, much like Korea before it, the eventual attempts by the North to unify the country under Communist rule led to intervention by the US. On the home front, the **Vietnam War** became more and more unpopular politically, with Americans growing increasingly discontent with the inability of the US to achieve the goals it had set for the Asian country. When President **Richard Nixon** took office in 1969, his escalation of the war led to protests at Kent State in Ohio, during which several students were killed by National Guard troops. Protests continued, eventually resulting in the end of the compulsory draft in 1973. In that same year, the US departed Vietnam. In 1975, the South surrendered, and Vietnam became a unified country under communist rule.

Events of the Gerald Ford Presidency

Gerald Ford was appointed to the vice presidency after Nixon's vice president **Spiro Agnew** resigned in 1973 under charges of tax evasion. With Nixon's resignation, Ford became president.

Ford's presidency saw negotiations with Russia to limit nuclear arms, as well as struggles to deal with inflation, economic downturn, and energy shortages. Ford's policies sought to reduce governmental control of various businesses and reduce the role of government overall. He also worked to prevent escalation of conflicts in the Middle East.

End of the Cold War and the Dissolution of the Soviet Union

In the late 1980s, **Mikhail Gorbachev** led the Soviet Union. He introduced a series of reform programs. **Ronald Reagan** famously urged Gorbachev to tear down the **Berlin Wall** as a gesture of growing freedom in the Eastern Bloc, and in 1989 it was demolished, ending the separation of East and West Germany. The Soviet Union relinquished its power over the various republics in Eastern Europe, and they became independent nations with their own individual governments. In 1991, the **USSR** was dissolved and the Cold War also came to an end.

Review Video: The End of the Cold War
Visit mometrix.com/academy and enter code: 278032

Events of the Jimmy Carter Presidency

Jimmy Carter was elected as president in 1976. Faced with a budget deficit, high unemployment, and continued inflation, Carter also dealt with numerous matters of international diplomacy, including:

- **Torrijos-Carter Treaties**—the US gave control of the Panama Canal to Panama.
- **Camp David Accords**—negotiations between Anwar el-Sadat, the president of Egypt, and Menachem Begin, the Israeli Prime Minister, led to a peace treaty between Egypt and Israel.
- **Strategic Arms Limitation Talks (SALT)**—these led to agreements and treaties between the US and the Soviet Union.
- **Iran Hostage Crisis**—after the Shah of Iran was deposed, an Islamic cleric, Ayatollah Khomeini, came to power. The shah came to the US for medical treatment, and Iran demanded his return so he could stand trial. In retaliation, a group of Iranian students stormed the US Embassy in Iran. Fifty-two American hostages were held for 444 days.

Jimmy Carter was awarded the **Nobel Peace Prize** in 2002.

Events of the Ronald Reagan Presidency

Ronald Reagan, at 69, became the oldest American president. The two terms of his administration included notable events such as:

- Reaganomics, also known as supply-side, trickle-down, or free-market economics, involving major tax cuts
- Economic Recovery Tax Act of 1981
- First female justice appointed to the Supreme Court—Sandra Day O'Connor
- Massive increase in the national debt—from $1 trillion to $3 trillion

- Reduction of nuclear weapons via negotiations with Mikhail Gorbachev
- Iran-Contra scandal—cover-up of US involvement in revolutions in El Salvador and Nicaragua
- Deregulation of savings and loan industry
- Loss of the space shuttle *Challenger*

Events of the George H. W. Bush Presidency

Reagan's presidency was followed by a term under his former vice president, **George H. W. Bush**. Bush's run for president included the famous "**thousand points of light**" speech, which was instrumental in increasing his standing in the election polls. During Bush's presidency, numerous international events took place, including:

- Fall of the Berlin wall and Germany's unification
- Panamanian dictator Manuel Noriega captured and tried on drug and racketeering charges
- Dissolution of the Soviet Union
- Gulf War, or Operation Desert Storm, triggered by Iraq's invasion of Kuwait
- Tiananmen Square Massacre in Beijing, China
- Ruby Ridge
- The arrival of the World Wide Web

Events of the William Clinton Presidency

William Jefferson "Bill" Clinton was the second president in US history to be impeached, but he was not convicted, and maintained high approval ratings in spite of the impeachment. Major events during his presidency included:

- Family and Medical Leave Act
- "Don't Ask, Don't Tell," a compromise position regarding homosexuals serving in the military
- North American Free Trade Agreement, or NAFTA
- Defense of Marriage Act
- Oslo Accords
- Siege at Waco, Texas, involving the Branch Davidians led by David Koresh
- Bombing of the Murrah Federal Building in Oklahoma City, Oklahoma
- Troops sent to Haiti, Bosnia, and Somalia to assist with domestic problems in those areas

Events of the George W. Bush Presidency

George W. Bush, son of George H. W. Bush, became president after Clinton. Major events during his presidency included:

- September 11, 2001, al-Qaeda terrorists hijack commercial airliners and fly into the World Trade Center towers and the Pentagon, killing nearly 3,000 Americans
- US troops sent to Afghanistan to hunt down al-Qaeda leaders, including the head of the organization, Osama Bin Laden; beginning of the War on Terror
- US troops sent to Iraq, along with a multinational coalition, to depose Saddam Hussein and prevent his deployment of suspected weapons of mass destruction
- Subprime mortgage crisis and near collapse of the financial industry, leading to the Great Recession; first of multiple government bailouts of the financial industry

Events of the Barack Obama Presidency

In 2008, Barack Obama, a senator from Illinois, became the first African American US president. His administration focused on improving the lot of a country suffering from a major recession. His major initiatives included:

- Economic bailout packages
- Improvements in women's rights
- Moves to broaden LGBT rights
- Health care reform legislation
- Reinforcement of the war in Afghanistan

Events of the Donald Trump Presidency

In 2016, Donald Trump, previously a real estate developer and television personality, was elected 45th president after a tumultuous election in which he won the electoral college but lost the popular vote. Marked by tension between the administration and domestic media, Trump's initiatives included:

- Appointing three Supreme Court Justices: Neil Gorsuch, Brett Kavanaugh, and Amy Coney Barrett
- Passing a major tax reform bill
- Enacting travel and emigration restrictions on eight nations: Iran, Libya, Syria, Yemen, Somalia, Chad, North Korea, and Venezuela
- Recognizing Jerusalem, rather than Tel Aviv, as the capital of Israel
- Responding to the novel coronavirus (SARS-CoV-2) outbreak

Almost completely along party lines, Donald Trump was impeached by the House on charges of abuse of power and obstruction of Congress; he was acquitted by the Senate.

Chapter Quiz

Ready to see how well you retained what you just read? Scan the QR code to go directly to the chapter quiz interface for this study guide. If you're using a computer, simply visit the online resources page at **mometrix.com/resources719/ssregushistgov** and click the Chapter Quizzes link.

Geography and Culture

Anthropology, Sociology, and Psychology

Importance of Socialization to Individuals Within a Specific Culture

Individuals learn how to function within a specific culture, group, or society via a process called **socialization**. Social contact with other human beings is vitally important to early development so that children can grow up to function in society as expected.

During the early years, children receive socialization from their families, siblings, peers, and schoolmates, as well as from exposure to mass media when applicable. Observing the behavior of others and adapting it to their own use helps children learn to interact with others. This process continues throughout life as individuals learn to adapt to various situations and interact with new groups.

Processes That Bring Cultural Change and Traits That Appear in All Cultures

Three major processes bring about the majority of changes in a culture:

1. **Discovery**—finding things that already exist, such as fire, a major cultural transformer
2. **Invention**—creating new equipment, machinery, etc., that changes the way tasks are accomplished
3. **Diffusion**—borrowing elements from other cultures

Over 70 **traits** have been identified that are found in nearly every culture to some level. These traits can be divided into four categories that determine the basic structure, mores, norms, and other characteristics of a culture:

- Language and cognition
- Society
- Myth, ritual, and aesthetics
- Technology

Culture

Culture refers to all learned human behaviors and behavioral patterns and is made up of:

- **Cultural universals**—traits shared by all human beings, such as language
- **Culture**—all traditions that define a society
- **Subculture**—groups within a culture that share specific traits

While culture serves as a survival mechanism by bringing people together in groups and helping individuals identify with each other, it also undergoes frequent and sometimes profound **change** as groups respond to new technologies, knowledge, or contact with other cultures.

Characteristics and Importance of Religion in an Anthropological Sense

Strictly defined, **religion** consists of a belief system and usually a set of rituals involving worship of a supernatural force or forces that have some effect on both everyday life and the overall structure and functioning of the world around us. Religion provides meaning and explanation for various life events and profoundly affects a culture's **worldviews**. Religion provides emotional support for individuals and a sense of **community** within a group that has shared religious views. Religious organization also provides structured sets of **moral norms** and motivation to abide by these norms and rules.

Increased **secularization**, particularly in developed countries, has reduced the role of religion in everyday life, leading individuals to find other systems to fill these basic human needs.

Behaviorism

John B. Watson, an American, developed the idea of **behaviorism**. In his theory, growth, learning, and training would always win out over any possible inborn tendencies. He believed that any person, regardless of origin, could learn to perform any type of art, craft, or enterprise with sufficient training and experience.

Science of Sociology

Sociology is a scientific discipline that focuses on the study of societies. Human societies are made up of institutions, groups, and individuals. How all these levels of organization **interact** is the major interest of sociologists. The way individuals organize themselves, how they interact with each other, and the attitudes and beliefs different groups develop all define those groups' cultural backgrounds. Groups of people in the same geographical area often develop similar organizational structures, beliefs, and attitudes.

Impact of Technology and Media on Culture

Technology is one of the primary means through which culture is developed, exchanged, spread, and experienced. Historically, the introduction of new technologies have made culture more accessible to people. An early example of this is the printing press, which allowed cultural products, such as poetry, novels, and histories, to be accessed by people outside of the elite and rich classes. In the modern era, the invention of the internet and propagation of social media has led to the world's cultures becoming more interconnected than ever before. In addition to connecting people and providing access to certain elements of culture, the internet has bred its own unique cultural products, such as memes and online activism. While current technologies have connected the various cultures of the world, some social scientists believe that the internet and social media could lead to the homogenization of culture and the disappearance of tradition, as certain dominant cultures overpower others in the digital landscape.

Major Study Areas Covered by Sociology

The five major study areas covered by sociology are:

1. **Population studies**—these studies involve observing social patterns of groups of people who live in the same area.
2. **Social behaviors**—sociologists study how general behaviors change over time, as well as attitudes such as morale, need for conformity, and other elements of social interaction.
3. **Cultural influences**—the influences of culture on social groups include art, religion, language, and overall knowledge and learning.
4. **Social change**—this involves the ways societies change over time, including major events such as wars and revolutions, or the way technology changes how people interact.
5. **Social institutions**—large groups of people are organized to fit specific niches in society, such as churches, hospitals, government, businesses, and schools. These organizations change over time and according to the overall needs and beliefs of an individual society.

How Sociologists Gather and Test Data

The three major methods of gathering data for sociological studies are:

1. **Surveys**—gathering information via direct questioning of members of the social group being studied
2. **Controlled experiments**—performing experiments that change an element of society
3. **Field observations**—living among members of a particular group or culture and observing how they interact and live their everyday lives

Major Classifications of Social Groups

Social groups are defined based on how they come into being, how they develop, and how they interact with wider society. The five major classifications are:

1. **Primary groups**—focused on members' need for support, such as a family or friend grouping
2. **Secondary groups**—form around the need to complete a task
3. **Reference groups**—help form an individual's identity
4. **In-groups and out-groups**—oppose each other or exclude members of other groups
5. **Social networks**—provide multiple links to an often large number of other individuals

Major Types of Social Interaction

Five main forms of social interaction help define social groups:

1. Cooperation
2. Coercion
3. Conflict
4. Conformity
5. Social exchange

All of these elements can bring a group into existence, break it apart, or transform it.

Major Social Institutions that Characterize and Meet the Needs of Any Society

Six major social institutions that characterize and meet the needs of any society are:

1. **Family**—this is the basic unit of any society and the most important social institution in all sociological study.
2. **Education**—in many societies, the values and norms of culture are communicated through institutionalized education as well as via the family.
3. **Political institutions**—political institutions in a society determine the distribution of power.
4. **Economic institutions**—these institutions determine the distribution of wealth.
5. **Religion**—this provides mores and beliefs that help unify a culture. Unfortunately, many religions also function in an in-group/out-group capacity.
6. **Sport**—this reflects values of society, promotes unity, and provides an outlet for aggression.

Various Patterns to Define Relationships Involving Race and Ethnicity

In general, relationships within cultures involving race and ethnicity are defined by either assimilation or conflict. **Assimilation** in the US can involve:

- **Anglo-conformity**—immigrants and racial minorities conform to the expectations of Anglo-American society, whether by choice, necessity, or force.
- **Cultural pluralism**—this involves the acceptance of varieties of racial and ethnic groups.
- **Accommodation**—this is mutual adaptation between majority and minority groups.
- **Melting pot**—the mixing together of various ethnic groups will bring about a new cultural group.

Patterns of **conflict** include:

- **Population transfer**—one group is required or forced to leave by another group.
- **Subjugation**—one group exercises control over the other.
- **Genocide**—one group slaughters another.

Ways Gender and Age Lead to Discrimination

In spite of legislation, education, and other attempts to bring about a higher level of equality, **discrimination** still exists against women and the elderly, particularly as it involves law, politics, and economic standing. Discrimination against **women** is particularly profound in most developing countries. It is believed that increasing the standing of women in a society is a major element in increasing the overall livelihood of that society.

While some societies value the **elderly** for their knowledge and experience, others discriminate against older people because of their decreased physical ability and ability to contribute economically. In the US, the poverty level for the elderly still stands at about ten percent. As lifespan increases, all societies must find a way to accommodate the needs of the elderly population.

Importance of Auguste Comte

Auguste Comte, a French philosopher, first used the term *sociology* to describe the study of human organizations and culture. His major theory was **positivism**. Positivism relies entirely on physical and sensory data to describe and evaluate human experience, completely discounting anything metaphysical. **Social behavior**, according to Comte, could be measured scientifically, as could major events that occurred in different populations. Comte is considered to be the first sociologist in the Western world.

Influence of Émile Durkheim on Sociology and Sociological Study

Through Durkheim's efforts, sociology eventually came to be considered a discipline in major universities. Heavily influenced by Comte's views of positivism, Durkheim felt the larger world was influenced by group beliefs, attitudes, and cultural aspects rather than by individuals. He performed in-depth studies on the cause of higher suicide rates among certain social groups. In the course of this study, he discussed **anomie**, a condition when people are affected by larger changes in society, such as unemployment or alienation of social groups, and receive little moral guidance from society.

Philosophy of Karl Marx and Friedrich Engels

According to Marx and Engels, society worldwide could be boiled down to a constant struggle between **classes**. This socioeconomic battle, as explained in *The Communist Manifesto*, would eventually lead to a revolution by the working class, since work itself is a social organization that involves large groups of people.

Herbert Spencer

Herbert Spencer is credited with the idea known as **Social Darwinism**. Though he and Darwin were technically rivals, Spencer applied Darwin's idea of "**survival of the fittest**" (a term actually coined by Spencer) to the way society develops. According to Spencer, **competition** is the major driving force behind the development and changes inherent in human society.

Max Weber

Weber's major thesis stated that the differing **religions** of the East and West led to differences in societal development. Weber believed **Protestantism** as a religion influenced the development of **capitalism** in the West. He also stated that the organization of the state felt **violence** was a legitimate means of protecting citizenry or enforcing rule. Police action, military action, and violence of individuals against each other in order to protect themselves or property demonstrate the state's propensity to solve problems through violence.

Science of Anthropology

While archaeology studies the physical remains of populations, **anthropology,** in contrast, is the study of human culture, its development, and how various cultural groups are similar or different. Anthropologists often engage in direct study of cultures by living among them, observing and participating in everyday activities. This is referred to as "**participant observation**." Anthropologists also perform cross-cultural and comparative research.

Anthropology can be divided into four major areas of study. Each one addresses a slightly different approach to culture and how it affects human beings, as well as how culture develops over time:

- **Archaeology**—this is the study of materials and physical items left behind by human settlements
- **Social-cultural anthropology**—focuses on cultural standards, beliefs, values, and norms
- **Biological anthropology**—this is the study of specific genetic characteristics of different populations
- **Linguistics**— this is the study of the development of languages over time

Subsistence Patterns and Its Major Classifications

The term *subsistence pattern* refers to ways in which societies obtain the necessities of life, such as food and shelter. The **subsistence pattern** of a society often directly correlates to its economy, population size, political systems, and overall technological development. Certain subsistence patterns can only support lower levels of societal development, while others can support a much more developed culture. The four major subsistence patterns are:

1. **Foraging**—the hunter-gatherer lifestyle
2. Pastoralism—herding
3. **Horticulture**—small-scale farming
4. Intensive agriculture—large-scale farming

Hunter-gatherer societies by nature are nomadic and do not tend to support highly developed cultures. Intensive agriculture, in contrast, can support a large population to a high subsistence level, allowing for the development of a sophisticated, modern culture.

Evolution in Anthropology

Darwin's theory of evolution had considerable effects on early anthropology. One theory that was inspired by Darwin's work was cultural evolutionism, which in the 19th century was the idea that societies evolved from simpler to more complex forms in a unilinear fashion. Those who believed in this form of cultural evolution often turned to Darwin's theory of evolution as a biological analogue for the types of changes that cultures underwent; however, this unilinear theory of cultural evolutionism eventually fell out of favor due to its ethnocentrism and was replaced by a more nuanced, multilinear theory of cultural evolution.

ETHNOCENTRISM

Ethnocentrism is the conscious or unconscious cultural or ethnic bias in which someone views the world through his or her group's perspective, often resulting in placing that group above another group. One's group becomes the reference point to which other groups are compared. This can lead to inaccurate views of other groups and in-group/out-group bias. In anthropology, this has historically led to some European anthropologists viewing cultures from other parts of the world as being less developed or less sophisticated simply because their cultures differed from those of Europe.

CULTURAL RELATIVISM

Cultural relativism is the belief that cultural concepts and morals should be viewed within the cultural contexts in which they appear and should not be judged according to the standards of another culture. Franz Boas, an anthropologist, first developed this concept in the late 19th and early 20th centuries. He believed that civilization was relative and that the morals, laws, and standards of one society were not absolute.

MARGARET MEAD

Margaret Mead studied sexual beliefs and norms among **South Pacific** and **Southeast Asian** cultures. Her first book on the subject was *Coming of Age in Samoa*. She acquired a PhD from Columbia University, and her work popularized sociology. She studied how children were treated and brought up in different cultures and how breastfeeding was viewed in different population groups.

MARY AND LOUIS LEAKEY AND DISCOVERIES AT OLDUVAI GORGE

The Leakeys made major discoveries regarding the **origin of the human species** during their excavations in Olduvai Gorge in Tanzania, Africa, excavating wide varieties of stone tools and other artifacts dating back as far as two million years. Mary Leakey discovered footprints belonging to early humans at **Laetoli**, a palaeontological site in Tanzania, and developed a system to classify early human tools. The Leakeys also discovered prehistoric remains of humans, including early humans dating to nearly four million years ago, fifteen new species, and one new genus of early human ancestors. They also discovered the first fossil ape skull, and only three similar specimens exist to this day. Their findings fundamentally changed theories regarding the development and evolution of ancient humans.

PSYCHOLOGY

Psychology is the study of **human behavior** and how the **mind** works. Some psychologists pursue scientific psychology, while others focus on applied psychology. Psychologists correlate human behavior and can make use of this data to predict behavior or determine why a particular behavior has occurred. Psychologists also help work with people who have specific problems with relationships or with how they perceive the world. By observing patterns and recording them in detail, psychologists can apply these patterns to predictions about human behavior in individuals, groups, cultures, and even countries.

Techniques Used by Psychologists in Research

Psychological researchers study their discipline in various ways. Based on what they are studying, they generally use one of the following methods:

- **Naturalistic observation**—much as with sociological study, psychologists observe people and their natural behavior without interfering.
- **Survey method**—surveys are distributed among a wide range of people, and the answers are correlated.
- **Case studies**—specific individuals or groups are studied in depth over a period of time, sometimes for many years.
- **Experimental method**—this involves experimental and control groups and the use of specific experiments to prove or disprove a theory.
- **Correlational design**—this is concerned with relationships between variables, such as whether one factor causes or influences another.

Importance of Aristotle to the Science of Psychology

Aristotle is often cited as founding the science of **psychology** through his overall interest in the working of the human mind. His beliefs stated that the mind was part of the body, while the psyche functioned as a receiver of knowledge. He felt psychology's major focus was to uncover the soul. Later philosophers and scientists built on these ideas to eventually develop the modern science of psychology.

Nativism

Nativism is a theory that states that there is a certain **body of knowledge** all people are born with. This knowledge requires no learning or experience on the part of the individual. **René Descartes**, a French philosopher, developed this concept. He believed the body and mind affected each other profoundly, largely because they are separate from each other. The physical site of this interaction took place in the **pineal gland** (a small gland in the brain), according to his theory. Descartes developed several theories in the fields of philosophy and psychology that are still studied in modern universities.

Empiricism

Empiricism is in direct opposition to Descartes' theory of nativism, theorizing that all knowledge is acquired through **life experience**, impressing itself on a mind and brain that are **blank** at the time of birth. Major proponents of empiricism were Thomas Hobbes, John Locke, David Hume, and George Berkeley.

Johannes P. Müller, Hermann L. F. von Helmholtz, William James, and Wilhelm Wundt

Johannes P. Müller and Hermann L. F. von Helmholtz conducted scientific, organized studies of sensation and perception. As the first psychologists to attempt this kind of study, they showed that it was possible to study actual physical processes that work to produce mental activity.

William James was the founder of the world's first psychology laboratory. **Wilhelm Wundt**, a student of Helmholtz, published the first experimental psychology journal and is known as the father of modern psychology. Together, James and Wundt helped bring psychology into its own, separating it from philosophy. The method of psychological study called introspection grew out of their work.

Sigmund Freud

An Austrian doctor, Freud developed a number of theories regarding human mental processes and behavior. He believed the **subconscious** to hold numerous repressed experiences and feelings that drive behavior without the individual's awareness, and that these subconscious motivators could lead to severe personality problems and disorders. He particularly stressed sexual desire as a motivating force. Freud developed the method of **psychoanalysis** to help discover the hidden impulses driving individual behavior. Freud's psychoanalytic theory proposed three major components to an individual's psychological makeup:

- **Id**—driven by instinct and basic drives
- **Ego**—most conscious and producing self-awareness
- **Superego**—strives for perfection and appropriate behavior

The **ego** acts as mediator between the **id** and **superego**, which function in opposition to each other.

Review Video: Sigmund Freud
Visit mometrix.com/academy and enter code: 473747

Carl Jung

A student of Freud, Jung eventually developed different theories regarding the workings of the human mind. With an intense interest in both Eastern and Western philosophy, he incorporated ideas from both into his psychological explorations. He developed the theories of **extroversion** and **introversion**, as well as proposing the existence of the **collective unconscious** and the occurrence of **synchronicity**.

Cognitive Psychology

Cognitive psychology is the study of how the brain thinks, remembers, processes information, and learns. It developed as a departure from behaviorism and focuses on internal mental processes instead of observable behaviors. Cognitive psychologists investigate higher-order mental processes and how they contribute to our thinking and emotions.

Humanistic Psychology

Humanistic psychology was developed partially as a response to psychoanalysis and behaviorism, which previously dominated the field. It arose in the middle of the twentieth century and emphasizes human potential and the ability for individuals to reach self-actualization. Humanist psychologists take a holistic approach to therapy and prioritize the experiences and desires of individuals rather than attempt to analyze their subconscious thoughts or change their behaviors. Humanist psychologists aim to help people achieve self-actualization through their relationships and personal insights.

Abraham Maslow

Abraham Maslow was an American humanist psychologist. His most notable contribution to the field of psychology was his hierarchy of needs. Maslow suggested that human needs were arranged in a hierarchy. At the bottom of the hierarchy are physiological needs, such as breathing, eating, and sleeping. Above strictly physiological needs are the needs for safety, love, and self-esteem. At the top of the hierarchy is self-actualization, which involves morality, creativity, acceptance, meaning, and reaching one's potential. The lower needs must usually be met before focus can be placed on the higher needs, but Maslow admitted that there is often some overlap in the real world.

Ivan Pavlov and B. F. Skinner

Ivan Pavlov and B. F. Skinner both built on Watson's theories of behaviorism. This work came about largely as a counter to the growing importance of introspective techniques to psychological study. Believing **environment** strongly influenced individual behavior, Pavlov and Skinner searched for connections between outside stimuli and behavioral patterns. Pavlov's experiments proved the existence of **conditioned response**. His most famous experiment conditioned dogs to salivate at the sound of a ringing bell. Skinner went on to build further on these ideas, developing the "Skinner box," a device used to develop and study conditioned response in rats.

Gestalt Psychology, Social Psychology, and Modern Psychology

Gestalt psychology is a school of psychology that was developed in the 20th century by **Max Wertheimer, Kurt Koffka, and Wolfgang Kohler**. In **Gestalt theory**, events are not considered individually but as part of a larger pattern. **Social psychology** is the study of how social conditions affect individuals. **Modern psychology**, as it has developed, combines earlier schools of psychology, including Freudian, Jungian, behaviorism, cognitive, humanistic, and stimulus-response theories.

Divisions of the Human Lifespan

Developmental psychologists divide the human lifespan into stages and list certain developmental milestones that generally take place during these stages:

- **Infancy and childhood**—this is the most rapid period of human development, during which the child learns to experience its world, relate to other people, and perform tasks necessary to function in its native culture. Debate exists as to which characteristics are inborn and which are learned.
- **Adolescence**—this period represents the shift from child to adult. Changes are rapid and can involve major physical and emotional shifts.
- **Adulthood**—individuals take on new responsibilities, become self-sufficient, and often form their own families and other social networks.
- **Old age**—priorities shift again as children become adults and no longer require support and supervision.

Types of Learning

Psychologists define learning as a **permanent change in behavior**. Learning is divided into three basic categories, based on how the behavioral change is acquired:

- **Classical conditioning**—this is a learning process in which a specific stimulus is associated with a specific response over time.
- **Operant conditioning**—this is a learning process in which behavior is punished or rewarded, leading to a desired long-term behavior.
- **Social learning**—this refers to learning based on observation of others and modeling others' behavior.

These three learning processes work together to produce the wide variety of human behavior.

Factors Involved in Social Psychology and Effects on Various Groups of People

Social psychology studies how people **interact** as well as why and how they decide whom to interact with. The ways people react with each other are defined in several ways, including:

- **Social perception**—this describes how we perceive others and their behavior as we make judgments based on our own experiences and prejudices.
- **Personal relationships**—close relationships develop among people for various reasons, including the desire to reproduce and form a family unit.
- **Group behavior**—people gather into groups with similar beliefs, needs, or other characteristics. Sometimes group behavior differs greatly from behavior that would be practiced by individuals.
- **Attitudes**—individual attitudes toward others develop over time based on individual history, experience, knowledge, and other factors. Attitudes can change over time, but some are deeply ingrained and can lead to prejudice.

Chapter Quiz

Ready to see how well you retained what you just read? Scan the QR code to go directly to the chapter quiz interface for this study guide. If you're using a computer, simply visit the online resources page at **mometrix.com/resources719/ssregushistgov** and click the Chapter Quizzes link.

Government and Citizenship

US Government and Citizenship

Political Science and Its Ties to Other Major Disciplines

Political science focuses on studying different governments and how they compare to each other, general political theory, ways political theory is put into action, how nations and governments interact with each other, and a general study of governmental structure and function. Other elements of **political science** include the study of elections, governmental administration at various levels, development and action of political parties, and how values such as freedom, power, justice, and equality are expressed in different political cultures. Political science also encompasses elements of other disciplines, including:

- **History**—how historical events have shaped political thought and process
- **Sociology**—the effects of various stages of social development on the growth and development of government and politics
- **Anthropology**—the effects of governmental process on the culture of an individual group and its relationships with other groups
- **Economics**—how government policies regulate the distribution of products and how they can control and/or influence the economy in general

General Political Theory

Based on general political theory, the four major purposes of any given government are:

- **Ensuring national security**—the government protects against international, domestic, and terrorist attacks and also ensures ongoing security through negotiating and establishing relationships with other governments.
- **Providing public services**—the government should "promote the general welfare," as stated in the Preamble to the US Constitution, by providing whatever is needed to its citizens.
- **Ensuring social order**—the government supplies means of settling conflicts among citizens as well as making laws to govern the nation, state, or city.
- **Making decisions regarding the economy**—laws help form the economic policy of the country, regarding both domestic and international trade and related issues. The government also has the ability to distribute goods and wealth to some extent among its citizens.

Main Theories Regarding the Origin of the State

There are four main theories regarding the origin of the state:

- **Evolutionary**—the state evolved from the family, with the head of state the equivalent of the family's patriarch or matriarch.
- **Force**—one person or group of people brought everyone in an area under their control, forming the first government.
- **Divine Right**—certain people were chosen by the prevailing deity to be the rulers of the nation, which is itself created by the deity or deities.

- **Social Contract**—there is no natural order. The people allow themselves to be governed to maintain social order, while the state, in turn, promises to protect the people they govern. If the government fails to protect its people, the people have the right to seek new leaders.

Public Policy

Public policy is the study of how the various levels of government formulate and implement policies. **Public policy** also refers to the set of policies that a government adopts and implements, including laws, plans, actions, and behaviors, for the purpose of governing society. Public policy is developed and adapted through the process of **policy analysis**. Public policy analysis is the systematic evaluation of alternative means of reaching social goals. Public policy is divided into various policy areas, including domestic policy, foreign policy, healthcare policy, education policy, criminal policy, national defense policy, and energy policy.

Influences of Philosophers on Political Study

Ancient Greek philosophers **Aristotle** and **Plato** believed political science would lead to order in political matters and that this scientifically organized order would create stable, just societies.

- **Thomas Aquinas** adapted the ideas of Aristotle to a Christian perspective. His ideas stated that individuals should have certain rights but also certain duties, and that these rights and duties should determine the type and extent of government rule. In stating that laws should limit the role of government, he laid the groundwork for ideas that would eventually become modern constitutionalism.
- **Niccolò Machiavelli**, author of *The Prince*, was a proponent of politics based on power. He is often considered the founder of modern political science.
- **Thomas Hobbes**, author of *Leviathan* (1651), believed that individuals' lives were focused solely on a quest for power and that the state must work to control this urge. Hobbes felt that people were completely unable to live harmoniously without the intervention of a powerful, undivided government.

Contributions of John Locke, Montesquieu, and Rousseau to Political Science

John Locke published *Two Treatises of Government* in 1689. This work argued against the ideas of Thomas Hobbes. He put forth the theory of *tabula rasa*—that people are born with minds like blank slates. Individual minds are molded by experience, not innate knowledge or intuition. He also believed that all men should be independent and equal. Many of Locke's ideas found their way into the Constitution of the United States.

The two French philosophers, **Montesquieu** and **Rousseau**, heavily influenced the French Revolution (1789-1799). They believed government policies and ideas should change to alleviate existing problems, an idea referred to as "liberalism." Rousseau, in particular, directly influenced the Revolution with writings such as *The Social Contract* (1762) and *Declaration of the Rights of Man and of the Citizen* (1789). Other ideas Rousseau and Montesquieu espoused included:

- Individual freedom and community welfare are of equal importance
- Man's innate goodness leads to natural harmony
- Reason develops with the rise of civilized society
- Individual citizens carry certain obligations to the existing government

Political Ideologies of Famous Philosophers

David Hume and **Jeremy Bentham** believed politics should have as its main goal maintaining "the greatest happiness for the greatest number." Hume also believed in empiricism, or that ideas should not be believed until the proof has been observed. He was a natural skeptic and always sought out the truth of matters rather than believing what he was told.

John Stuart Mill, a British philosopher and economist, made significant contributions to the fields of social and economic theory. A majorly influential thinker in the realm of classical liberalism, Mill believed in progressive policies such as women's suffrage, emancipation, and the development of labor unions and farming cooperatives. His ideas on free speech and the harm principle were the basis for the "clear and present danger" test outlined by Oliver Wendell Holmes Jr. when determining if speech is protected by the First Amendment of the US Constitution.

Johann Fichte and **Georg Hegel**, German philosophers in the late 18th and early 19th centuries, supported a form of liberalism grounded largely in socialism and a sense of nationalism.

Main Political Orientations

The four main political orientations are:

- **Liberal**—liberals believe that government should work to increase equality, even at the expense of some freedoms. Government should assist those in need, focusing on enforced social justice and free basic services for everyone.
- **Conservative**—a conservative believes that government should be limited in most cases. The government should allow its citizens to help one another and solve their own problems rather than enforcing solutions. Business should not be overregulated, allowing a free market.
- **Moderate**—this ideology incorporates some liberal and some conservative values, generally falling somewhere between in overall belief.
- **Libertarian**—libertarians believe that the government's role should be limited to protecting the life and liberty of citizens. Government should not be involved in any citizen's life unless that citizen is encroaching upon the rights of another.

Major Principles of Government as Outlined in the United States Constitution

The six major principles of government as outlined in the United States Constitution are:

- **Federalism**—the power of the government does not belong entirely to the national government but is divided between federal and state governments.
- **Popular sovereignty**—the government is determined by the people and gains its authority and power from the people.
- **Separation of powers**—the government is divided into three branches (executive, legislative, and judicial) with each having its own set of powers.
- **Judicial review**—courts at all levels of government can declare laws invalid if they contradict the constitutions of individual states, or the US Constitution, with the Supreme Court serving as the final judicial authority on decisions of this kind.
- **Checks and balances**—no single branch can act without input from another, and each branch has the power to "check" any other, as well as balance other branches' powers.
- **Limited government**—governmental powers are limited, and certain individual rights are defined as inviolable by the government.

Types of Powers Delegated to the National Government by the US Constitution

The structure of the US government divides power between national and state governments. Powers delegated to the federal government by the Constitution are:

- **Expressed powers**—powers directly defined in the Constitution, including power to declare war, regulate commerce, make money, and collect taxes
- **Implied powers**—powers the national government must have in order to carry out the expressed powers
- **Inherent powers**—powers inherent to any government, not expressly defined in the Constitution

Some of these powers, such as collection and levying of taxes, are also granted to the individual state governments.

Primary Positions of Federalism and Development through the Years in the US

The way federalism should be practiced has been the subject of debate since the writing of the Constitution. There were—and still are—two main factions regarding this issue:

- **States' rights**—those favoring the states' rights position feel that the state governments should take the lead in performing local actions to manage various problems.
- **Nationalist**—those favoring a nationalist position feel the national government should take the lead to deal with those same matters.

The flexibility of the Constitution has allowed the US government to shift and adapt as the needs of the country have changed. Power has often shifted from the state governments to the national government and back again, and both levels of government have developed various ways to influence each other.

Effects of Federalism on Policy-Making and the Balance of Politics in the US

Federalism has three major effects on **public policy** in the US:

- Determining whether the local, state, or national government originates policy
- Affecting how policies are made
- Ensuring policy-making functions under a set of limitations

Federalism also influences the **political balance of power** in the US by:

- Making it difficult, if not impossible, for a single political party to seize total power
- Ensuring that individuals can participate in the political system at various levels
- Making it possible for individuals working within the system to be able to affect policy at some level, whether local or more widespread

Three Branches of the US Federal Government

The following are the three branches of the US Federal government and the individuals that belong to each branch:

- **Legislative Branch**—this consists of the two houses of Congress: the House of Representatives and the Senate. All members of the Legislative Branch are elected officials.
- **Executive Branch**—this branch is made up of the president, vice president, presidential advisors, and other various cabinet members. Advisors and cabinet members are appointed by the president, but they must be approved by Congress.
- **Judicial Branch**—the federal court system, headed by the Supreme Court.

Review Video: What Does the Executive Branch Do?
Visit mometrix.com/academy and enter code: 210629

Review Video: What Does the Judicial Branch Do?
Visit mometrix.com/academy and enter code: 278093

Review Video: What Does the Legislative Branch Do?
Visit mometrix.com/academy and enter code: 405303

Major Responsibilities of the Three Branches of the Federal Government

The three branches of the federal government each have specific roles and responsibilities:

- The **Legislative Branch** is largely concerned with lawmaking. All laws must be approved by Congress before they go into effect. They are also responsible for regulating money and trade, approving presidential appointments, and establishing organizations like the postal service and federal courts. Congress can also propose amendments to the Constitution, and can impeach, or bring charges against, the president. Only Congress can declare war.
- The **Executive Branch** carries out laws, treaties, and war declarations enacted by Congress. The president can also veto bills approved by Congress, and serves as commander in chief of the US military. The president appoints cabinet members, ambassadors to foreign countries, and federal judges.

- The **Judicial Branch** makes decisions on challenges as to whether laws passed by Congress meet the requirements of the US Constitution. The Supreme Court may also choose to review decisions made by lower courts to determine their constitutionality.

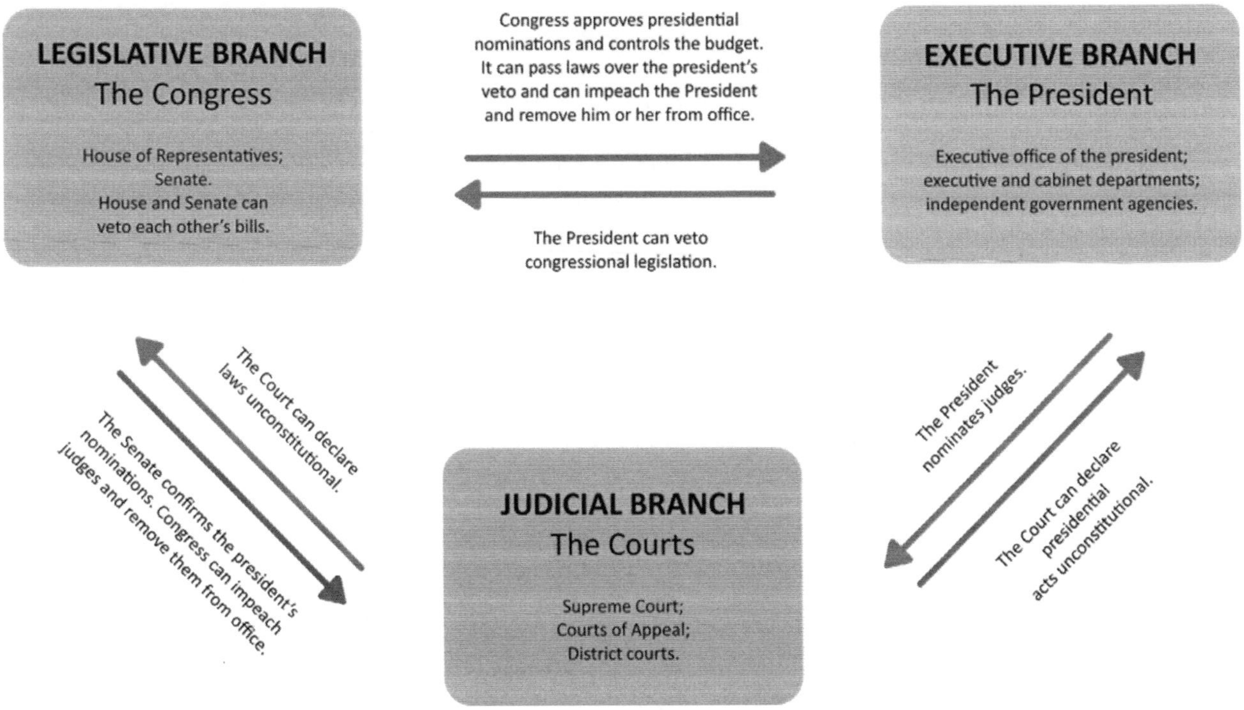

US Citizenship

Qualifications of a US citizen/How Citizenship May Be Lost

Anyone born in the US, born abroad to a US citizen, or who has gone through a process of naturalization is considered a **citizen** of the United States. It is possible to lose US citizenship as a result of conviction of certain crimes such as treason. Citizenship may also be lost if a citizen pledges an oath to another country or serves in the military of a country engaged in hostilities with the US. A US citizen can also choose to hold dual citizenship, work as an expatriate in another country without losing US citizenship, or even to renounce citizenship if he or she so chooses.

Rights, Duties, and Responsibilities Granted to or Expected from Citizens

Citizens are granted certain rights under the US government. The most important of these are defined in the **Bill of Rights**, and include freedom of speech, religion, assembly, and a variety of other rights the government is not allowed to remove. A US citizen also has a number of **duties**:

- Paying taxes
- Loyalty to the government (though the US does not prosecute those who criticize or seek to change the government)
- Support and defense of the Constitution
- Serving in the Armed Forces when required by law
- Obeying laws as set forth by the various levels of government.

Responsibilities of a US citizen include:

- Voting in elections
- Respecting one another's rights and not infringing on them

- Staying informed about various political and national issues
- Respecting one another's beliefs

Bill of Rights

Importance of the Bill of Rights

The first ten amendments of the US Constitution are known as the **Bill of Rights**. These amendments prevent the government from infringing upon certain freedoms that the Founding Fathers felt were natural rights that already belonged to all people. These rights included freedom of speech, freedom of religion, freedom of assembly, and the right to bear arms. Many of the rights were formulated in direct response to the way the colonists felt they had been mistreated by the British government.

Rights Granted in the Bill of Rights

The first ten amendments were passed by Congress in 1789. Three-fourths of the existing thirteen states had ratified them by December of 1791, making them official additions to the Constitution. The rights granted in the Bill of Rights are:

- **First Amendment**—freedom of religion, speech, freedom of the press, and the right to assemble and to petition the government
- **Second Amendment**—the right to bear arms
- **Third Amendment**—Congress cannot force individuals to house troops
- **Fourth Amendment**—protection from unreasonable search and seizure
- **Fifth Amendment**—no individual is required to testify against himself, and no individual may be tried twice for the same crime
- **Sixth Amendment**—the right to criminal trial by jury and the right to legal counsel
- **Seventh Amendment**—the right to civil trial by jury
- **Eighth Amendment**—protection from excessive bail or cruel and unusual punishment
- **Ninth Amendment**—prevents rights not explicitly named in the Constitution from being taken away because they are not named
- **Tenth Amendment**—any rights not directly delegated to the national government, or not directly prohibited by the government from the states, belong to the states or to the people

Review Video: Bill of Rights
Visit mometrix.com/academy and enter code: 585149

Situations Where the Government Restricts the First Amendment Freedoms

In some cases, the government restricts certain elements of First Amendment rights. Some examples include:

- **Freedom of religion**—when a religion espouses illegal activities, the government often restricts these forms of religious expression. Examples include polygamy, animal sacrifice, and use of illicit drugs or illegal substances.
- **Freedom of speech**—this can be restricted if exercise of free speech endangers other people.
- **Freedom of the press**—laws prevent the press from publishing falsehoods.

In **emergency situations** such as wartime, stricter restrictions are sometimes placed on these rights, especially rights to free speech and assembly, and freedom of the press, in order to protect national security.

Constitution's Address of the Rights of Those Accused of Crimes

The US Constitution makes allowances for the **rights of criminals**, or anyone who has transgressed established laws. There must be laws to protect citizens from criminals, but those accused of crimes must also be protected and their basic rights as individuals preserved. In addition, the Constitution protects individuals from the power of authorities to prevent police forces and other enforcement organizations from becoming oppressive. The fourth, fifth, sixth, and eighth amendments specifically address these rights.

Supreme Court's Provision of Equal Protection for All Individuals

When the Founding Fathers wrote in the Declaration of Independence that "all men are created equal," they actually were referring to men, and, in fact, defined citizens as white men who owned land. However, as the country has developed and changed, the definition has expanded to more wholly include all people.

"**Equality**" does not mean all people are inherently the same, but it does mean they all should be granted the same rights and should be treated the same by the government. Amendments to the Constitution have granted citizenship and voting rights to all Americans regardless of race or gender. The Supreme Court evaluates various laws and court decisions to determine if they properly represent the idea of **equal protection**. One sample case was Brown v. Board of Education in 1954, which declared separate-but-equal treatment to be unconstitutional.

Protests

A protest is an expression of opposition to, and sometimes of support of, events or circumstances. **Protests** represent a means for individuals to publicly make their views heard in an effort to influence public opinion or government policy, or as a means to enact **change**. Protests generally result when self-expression of opposing views is restricted by government policy, political or economic circumstances, religion, social structures, or the media, and people react by declaring their views through cultural mechanisms or on the streets. There are numerous forms of protest, including boycotts, civil disobedience, demonstrations, non-violent protests, picketing, protest marches, protest songs, riots, sit-ins, teach-ins, strikes, and others.

Civil Liberty Challenges Addressed in Current Political Discussions

The **civil rights movements** of the 1960s and the ongoing struggle for the rights of women and other minorities have sparked **challenges to existing law**. In addition, debate has raged over how much information the government should be required to divulge to the public. Major issues in the 21st century political climate include:

- Continued debate over women's rights, especially regarding equal pay for equal work
- Debate over affirmative action to encourage hiring of minorities
- Debate over civil rights of homosexuals, including marriage and military service
- Decisions as to whether minorities should be compensated for past discriminatory practices
- Balance between the public's right to know and the government's need to maintain national security
- Balance between the public's right to privacy and national security

Civil Liberties vs. Civil Rights

While the terms *civil liberties* and *civil rights* are often used interchangeably, in actuality, their definitions are slightly different. The two concepts work together, however, to define the basics of a free state:

- **"Civil liberties"** define the constitutional freedoms guaranteed to citizens. Examples include freedoms such as free speech, privacy, or free thought.
- **"Civil rights"** are guarantees of or protections of civil liberties. One comparison can be found in the case of freedom of religion. The civil liberty is that one has the freedom to practice the religion of his or her choice, whereas the civil right would protect that individual from being denied a job on the basis of their religion.

Suffrage, Franchise, and the Change of Voting Rights Over American History

Suffrage and franchise both refer to the right to **vote**. As the US developed as a nation, there was much debate over which individuals should hold this right. In the early years, only white male landowners were granted suffrage. By the 19th century, most states had franchised, or granted the right to vote, to all adult white males. The **Fifteenth Amendment** of 1870 granted suffrage to formerly enslaved men. The **Nineteenth Amendment** gave women the right to vote in 1920, and in 1971 the **Twenty-sixth Amendment** expanded voting rights to include any US citizen over the age of eighteen. However, those who have not been granted full citizenship and citizens who have committed certain crimes do not have voting rights.

Ways in Which the Voting Process Has Changed Over the Years

The first elections in the US were held by **public ballot**. However, election abuses soon became common, since public ballot made it easy to intimidate, threaten, or otherwise influence the votes of individuals or groups of individuals. New practices were put into play, including **registering voters** before elections took place and using a **secret or Australian ballot**. In 1892, the introduction of the **voting machine** further privatized the voting process, since it allowed complete privacy for voting. Today, debate continues about the accuracy of various voting methods, including high-tech voting machines and even low-tech punch cards.

Effect of Political Parties on the Functioning of an Individual Government

Different types and numbers of political parties can have a significant effect on how a government is run. If there is a **single party**, or a one-party system, the government is defined by that one party, and all policy is based on that party's beliefs. In a **two-party system**, two parties with different viewpoints compete for power and influence. The US is basically a two-party system, with checks and balances to make it difficult for one party to gain complete power over the other. There are also **multiparty systems**, with three or more parties. In multiparty systems, various parties will often come to agreements in order to form a majority and shift the balance of power.

Development of Political Parties in the US.

George Washington was adamantly against the establishment of **political parties**, based on the abuses perpetrated by such parties in Britain. However, political parties developed in US politics almost from the beginning. Major parties throughout US history have included:

- **Federalists and Democratic-Republicans**—these parties formed in the late 1700s and disagreed on the balance of power between national and state government.
- **Democrats and Whigs**—these developed in the 1830s, and many political topics of the time centered on national economic issues.
- **Democrats and Republicans**—the Republican Party developed before the Civil War, after the collapse of the Whig party, and the two parties debated issues centering on slavery and economic issues, such as taxation.

While third parties sometimes enter the picture in US politics, the government is basically a two-party system, dominated by the Democrats and Republicans.

Functions of Political Parties

Political parties form organizations at all levels of government. Activities of individual parties include:

- Recruiting and backing candidates for offices
- Discussing various issues with the public, increasing public awareness
- Working toward compromise on difficult issues
- Staffing government offices and providing administrative support

At the administrative level, parties work to ensure that viable candidates are available for elections and that offices and staff are in place to support candidates as they run for office and afterward, when they are elected.

Processes of Selecting Political Candidates

Historically, in the quest for political office, a potential candidate has followed one of the following four processes:

- **Nominating convention**—an official meeting of the members of a party for the express purpose of nominating candidates for upcoming elections. The Democratic National Convention and the Republican National Convention, convened to announce candidates for the presidency, are examples of this kind of gathering.
- **Caucus**—a meeting, usually attended by a party's leaders. Some states still use caucuses, but not all.
- **Primary election**—the most common method of choosing candidates today, the primary is a publicly held election to choose candidates.
- **Petition**—signatures gathered to place a candidate on the ballot. Petitions can also be used to place legislation on a ballot.

Ways the Average Citizen Participates in the Political Process

In addition to voting for elected officials, American citizens are able to participate in the political process through several other avenues. These include:

- Participating in local government
- Participating in caucuses for large elections

- Volunteering to help political parties
- Running for election to local, state, or national offices

Individuals can also donate money to political causes or support political groups that focus on specific causes such as abortion, wildlife conservation, or women's rights. These groups often make use of **representatives** who lobby legislators to act in support of their efforts.

Ways in Which Political Campaign Gains Funding

Political campaigns are very expensive. In addition to the basic necessities of a campaign office, including office supplies, office space, etc., a large quantity of the money that funds a political campaign goes toward **advertising**. Money to fund a political campaign can come from several sources, including:

- The candidate's personal funds
- Donations by individuals
- Special interest groups

The most significant source of campaign funding is **special interest groups**. Groups in favor of certain policies will donate money to candidates they believe will support those policies. Special interest groups also do their own advertising in support of candidates they endorse.

Presidential Elections

The President of the United States is elected **indirectly** by members of an **electoral college**. Members of the electoral college nearly always vote along the lines of the popular vote of their respective states. The winner of a presidential election is the candidate with at least 270 **Electoral College votes**. It is possible for a candidate to win the electoral vote and lose the popular vote. Incumbent Presidents and challengers typically prefer a balanced ticket, where the President and Vice President are elected together and generally balance one another with regard to geography, ideology, or experience working in government. The nominated Vice Presidential candidate is referred to as the President's **running mate**.

Importance of Free Press and the Media

The right to free speech guaranteed in the first amendment to the Constitution allows the media to report on **government and political activities** without fear of retribution. Because the media has access to information about the government, the government's policies and actions, and debates and discussions that occur in Congress, it can keep the public informed about the inner workings of the government. The media can also draw attention to injustices, imbalances of power, and other transgressions the government or government officials might commit. However, media outlets may, like special interest groups, align themselves with certain political viewpoints and skew their reports to fit that viewpoint. The rise of the **internet** has made media reporting even more complex, as news can be found from an infinite variety of sources, both reliable and unreliable.

Forms of Government

Anarchism, Communism, and Dictatorship

Anarchists believe that all government should be eliminated and that individuals should rule themselves. Historically, anarchists have used violence and assassination to further their beliefs.

Communism is based on class conflict, revolution, and a one-party state. Ideally, a communist government would involve a single government for the entire world. Communist government controls the production and flow of goods and services rather than leaving this to companies or individuals.

Dictatorship involves rule by a single individual. If rule is enforced by a small group, this is referred to as an oligarchy. Dictators tend to rule with a violent hand, using a highly repressive police force to ensure control over the populace.

Fascism and Monarchy

Fascism centers on a single leader and is, ideologically, an oppositional belief to communism. **Fascism** includes a single-party state and centralized control. The power of the fascist leader lies in the "cult of personality," and the fascist state often focuses on expansion and conquering of other nations. **Monarchy** was the major form of government for Europe through most of its history.

A monarchy is led by a king or a queen. This position is hereditary, and the rulers are not elected. In modern times, constitutional monarchy has developed, where the king and queen still exist, but most of the governmental decisions are made by democratic institutions such as a parliament.

Parliamentary and Democratic Systems

In a parliamentary system, government involves a legislature and a variety of political parties. The head of government, usually a prime minister, is typically the head of the dominant party. A head of state can be elected, or this position can be taken by a monarch, as in Great Britain's constitutional monarchy system.

In a **democratic system** of government, the people elect their government representatives. The word *democracy* is a Greek term that means "rule of the people." There are two forms of democracy: direct and indirect. In a direct democracy, each issue or election is decided by a vote where each individual is counted separately. An indirect democracy employs a legislature that votes on issues that affect large numbers of people whom the legislative members represent. Democracy can exist as a parliamentary system or a presidential system. The US is a presidential, indirect democracy.

Presidential System and Socialism

A presidential system, like a parliamentary system, has a legislature and political parties, but there is no difference between the head of state and the head of government. Instead of separating these functions, an elected president performs both. Election of the president can be direct or indirect, and the president may not necessarily belong to the largest political party. In **socialism**, the state controls the production of goods, though it does not necessarily own all means of production. The state also provides a variety of social services to citizens and helps guide the economy. A democratic form of government often exists in socialist countries.

Review Video: Communism vs. Socialism
Visit mometrix.com/academy and enter code: 917677

Totalitarian and Authoritarian Systems

A totalitarian system believes everything should be under the control of the government—from resource production, to the press, to religion, and other social institutions. All aspects of life under a totalitarian system must conform to the ideals of the government. **Authoritarian** governments practice widespread state authority but do not necessarily dismantle all public institutions. If a church, for example, exists as an organization but poses no threat to the authority of the state, an authoritarian government might leave it as it is. While all totalitarian governments are by definition authoritarian, a government can be authoritarian without becoming totalitarian.

Review Video: Totalitarianism vs. Authoritarianism
Visit mometrix.com/academy and enter code: 104046

Parliamentary and Democratic Systems

In a parliamentary system, government involves a legislature and a variety of political parties. The head of government, usually a prime minister, is typically the head of the dominant party. A head of state can be elected, or this position can be taken by a monarch, as in Great Britain's constitutional monarchy system.

In a **democratic system** of government, the people elect their government representatives. The word *democracy* is a Greek term that means "rule of the people." There are two forms of democracy: direct and indirect. In a direct democracy, each issue or election is decided by a vote where each individual is counted separately. An indirect democracy employs a legislature that votes on issues that affect large numbers of people whom the legislative members represent. Democracy can exist as a parliamentary system or a presidential system. The US is a presidential, indirect democracy.

Realism, Liberalism, Institutionalism, and Constructivism

The theory of realism states that nations are by nature aggressive and work in their own self-interest. Relations between nations are determined by military and economic strength. The nation is seen as the highest authority. **Liberalism** believes states can cooperate and that they act based on capability rather than power. This term was originally coined to describe Woodrow Wilson's theories on international cooperation. In **institutionalism**, institutions provide structure and incentive for cooperation among nations. Institutions are defined as a set of rules used to make international decisions. These institutions also help distribute power and determine how nations will interact. **Constructivism**, like liberalism, is based on international cooperation but recognizes that perceptions countries have of each other can affect their relations.

Effects of Foreign Policy on a Country's Position in World Affairs

Foreign policy is a set of goals, policies, and strategies that determine how an individual nation will interact with other countries. These strategies shift, sometimes quickly and drastically, according to actions or changes occurring in the other countries. However, a nation's **foreign policy** is often based on a certain set of ideals and national needs. Examples of US foreign policy include isolationism versus internationalism. In the 1800s, the US leaned more toward isolationism, exhibiting a reluctance to become involved in foreign affairs. The World Wars led to a period of internationalism, as the US entered these wars in support of other countries and joined the United Nations. Today's foreign policy tends more toward **interdependence**, or **globalism**, recognizing the widespread effects of issues like economic health.

Major Figures Involved in Determining and Enacting US Foreign Policy

US foreign policy is largely determined by Congress and the president, influenced by the secretary of state, secretary of defense, and the national security adviser. Executive officials carry out policies. The main departments in charge of these day-to-day issues are the **US Department of State**, also referred to as the State Department. The Department of State carries out policy, negotiates treaties, maintains diplomatic relations, assists citizens traveling in foreign countries, and ensures that the president is properly informed of any international issues. The **Department of Defense**, the largest executive department in the US, supervises the armed forces and provides assistance to the president in his role as commander-in-chief.

Major Types of International Organizations

Two types of international organizations are:

- **Intergovernmental organizations (IGOs)**. These organizations are made up of members from various national governments. The UN is an example of an intergovernmental organization. Treaties among the member nations determine the functions and powers of these groups.
- **Nongovernmental organizations (NGOs)**. An NGO lies outside the scope of any government and is usually supported through private donations. An example of an NGO is the International Red Cross, which works with governments all over the world when their countries are in crisis but is formally affiliated with no particular country or government.

Role of Diplomats in International Relations

Diplomats are individuals who reside in foreign countries in order to maintain communications between that country and their home country. They help negotiate trade agreements and environmental policies, as well as conveying official information to foreign governments. They also help to resolve conflicts between the countries, often working to sort out issues without making the conflicts official in any way. **Diplomats**, or **ambassadors**, are appointed in the US by the president. Appointments must be approved by Congress.

Role of the United Nations in International Relations and Diplomacy

The United Nations (**UN**) helps form international policies by hosting representatives of various countries who then provide input into policy decisions. Countries that are members of the UN must agree to abide by all final UN resolutions, but this is not always the case in practice, as dissent is not uncommon. If countries do not follow UN resolutions, the UN can decide on sanctions against those countries, often economic sanctions, such as trade restriction. The UN can also send military forces to problem areas, with "peacekeeping" troops brought in from member nations. An example of this function is the Korean War, the first war in which an international organization played a major role.

Landmark Supreme Court Cases and Civil Rights

Marbury v. Madison

Right before President **John Adams** left office after **Thomas Jefferson** won the presidency in the election of 1800, he passed the **Judiciary Act of 1801**. This act eliminated one seat on the Supreme Court, eliminated circuit duties for members of the Supreme Court, and created 16 federal circuit court judgeships. This allowed President John Adams to pack the federal court system with his fellow Federalists before Thomas Jefferson, a Democratic-Republican, took office. **William Marbury** was one of these individuals promised a position by John Adams. However, Adams's Secretary of State, **John Marshall**, did not have time to deliver Marbury's commission (which was the formal job offer for Marbury's position as Justice of the Peace for D.C.) before the Jefferson administration took over. The new Secretary of State, **James Madison**, refused to deliver Marbury's commission after he took office. This led to Marbury suing Madison for his commission, and the issue was brought before the Supreme Court in the case of ***Marbury v. Madison*** (1803).

Although Section XIII of the Judiciary Act of 1789 had a **Writ of Mandamus** which required Madison to honor the appointment, Chief Justice **John Marshall**, whom Adams appointed to the Supreme Court before leaving office, declared this section unconstitutional. This historic act established the doctrine of **judicial review**, which allows the Supreme Court to declare a legislative or executive act unconstitutional. Marshall thereby established an independent judiciary; he is quoted as saying, "The Constitution is the supreme Law of the Land, with the Supreme Court as the final interpreter."

McCulloch v. Maryland

When Congress chartered a national bank, the **Second Bank of the United States**, Maryland voted to tax any bank business dealing with banks chartered outside the state, including the federally chartered bank. Andrew McCulloch, an employee of the Second Bank of the US in Baltimore, refused to pay this tax. The resulting lawsuit from the State of Maryland went to the Supreme Court for judgment.

John Marshall, Chief Justice of the Supreme Court, stated that Congress was within its rights to charter a national bank. In addition, the State of Maryland did not have the power to levy a tax on the federal bank or on the federal government in general. In cases where state and federal government collided, precedent was set for the **federal government** to prevail.

The Civil Rights Act of 1871

The Civil Rights Act of 1871 was a statute passed following the Civil War. It was comprised of the **1870 Force Act** and the **1871 Ku Klux Klan Act**, and was passed primarily with the intention of protecting Southern black people from the Ku Klux Klan. Since it was passed in 1871, the statute has only undergone small changes. It has, however, been interpreted widely by the courts. In 1882, some parts of the Civil Rights Act of 1871 were found unconstitutional, but the Force Act and the Klan Act continued to be applied in civil rights cases in subsequent years.

Plessy v. Ferguson

Plessy v. Ferguson was an 1896 Supreme Court case. The case resulted in the decision that **de jure racial segregation** in **public facilities** was legal in the United States, and permitted states to restrict black people from using public facilities. The case originated when, in 1890, a black man named Homer Plessy decided to challenge a Louisiana law that segregated black and white people on trains by sitting in the white section of a train. Plessy was convicted of breaking the law in a Louisiana court, and the case was appealed to the US Supreme Court, where the Supreme Court upheld the Louisiana decision. The case established the legality of the doctrine of separate but equal, thereby allowing racial segregation. The decision was later overturned by **Brown v. the Board of Education of Topeka**.

The Fair Employment Act

The Fair Employment Act was signed by President Franklin Roosevelt in 1941. The purpose of the act was to **ban racial discrimination** in industries related to **national defense**, and it represented the very first federal law to ban discrimination in employment. The **Fair Employment Act** mandated that all federal government agencies and departments concerned with national defense, as well as private defense contractors, guaranteed that professional training would be conducted without discrimination based on race, creed, color, or national origin. The Fair Employment Act was followed by **Title VII of the 1964 Civil Rights Act**, which banned discrimination by private employers, and by **Executive Order 11246** in 1965, which concerned federal contractors and subcontractors.

Brown v. Board of Education

Brown versus the Board of Education of Topeka was a Supreme Court case that was decided in 1954. The case made it illegal for **racial segregation** to exist within **public education facilities**. This decision was based on the finding that separate but equal public educational facilities would not provide black and white students with the same standard of facilities. The case originated in

1951, when a lawsuit was filed by Topeka parents, who were recruited by the NAACP, against the Board of Education of the City of Topeka, Kansas in a US district court. The parents, one of whom was named Oliver Brown, wanted the Topeka Board of Education to eliminate racial segregation. The district court agreed that segregation had negative effects, but did not force the schools to desegregate because it found that black and white school facilities in the District were generally equal in standards. The case was appealed to the Supreme Court, where the finding was that separate educational facilities are unequal.

Bolling v. Sharpe

Bolling v. Sharpe was a 1954 Supreme Court case. Like Brown v. Board of Education, this case addressed issues concerning **segregation in public schools**. The case originated in 1949, when parents from Anacostia, an area in Washington, DC, petitioned the Board of Education of the District of Columbia to allow all races to attend a new school. The request was denied. A lawsuit was brought before the District Court for the District of Columbia on behalf of a student named Bolling and other students to admit them to the all-white school. The case was dismissed by the district court and taken to the Supreme Court. The Supreme Court ruled that the school had to be desegregated based on the Fifth Amendment.

Civil Rights Act of 1964

The Civil Rights Act of 1964 was passed to protect the rights of both **black men** and **women**. It served as part of the foundation for the women's rights movement. The act was a catalyst for change in the United States, as it made it illegal to engage in acts of **discrimination** in public facilities, in government, and in employment. The Civil Rights Act prohibited unequal voter registration, prohibited discrimination in all public facilities involved in interstate commerce, supported desegregating public schools, ensured equal protection for black people in federally funded programs, and banned employment discrimination.

The Pregnancy Discrimination Act

The Pregnancy Discrimination Act was passed in 1978 as an amendment to the sex discrimination clause of the Civil Rights Act of 1964. The **Pregnancy Discrimination Act** stipulated that people cannot be discriminated against due to pregnancy, childbirth, or medical issues related to pregnancy or childbirth. If a person becomes pregnant, gives birth, or has related medical conditions, they must receive treatment that is equivalent to that received by other employees and also receive equal benefits as other employees. The **Family and Medical Leave Act** was passed in 1993 to advance protections under the Pregnancy Discrimination Act.

Civil Rights Act of 1968

The Civil Rights Act of 1968 was passed following the passing of the Civil Rights Act of 1964. The act made it illegal to **discriminate** against individuals during the sale, rental, or financing of **housing**. Therefore, the act is also referred to as the **Fair Housing Act of 1968**. The act made it illegal to refuse to sell or rent housing based on race, color, religion, or national origin. It also made it illegal to advertise housing for sale or rent and to specify a preference to rent or sell the property to an individual of a particular race, color, religion, or national origin. In addition, the act ensured protection for civil rights workers.

Age Discrimination in Employment Act

The Age Discrimination in Employment Act of 1967 made it illegal for employers to discriminate against people who are **forty years old** or greater in age. The act establishes standards for employer-provided pensions and benefits, and mandates that information regarding the needs of older workers be made publicly available. In addition to generally banning age discrimination, the

ADEA specifies particular actions that are illegal. Employers may not specify that individuals of a certain age are preferred or are conversely restricted from applying to job ads. Age limits are only permitted to be mentioned in job ads if age has been shown to be a bona fide occupational qualification. The act stipulates that it is illegal to discriminate against age through apprenticeship programs and that it is illegal to restrict benefits to older employees. However, employers are permitted to lower the benefits provided to older employees based on age if the expense of providing fewer or lesser benefits is equivalent to the expense of providing benefits to younger employees.

Loving v. Virginia

Loving v. Virginia was a 1967 Supreme Court case that ruled that a particular law in Virginia known as the **Racial Integrity Act of 1924** was unconstitutional, as the law had prohibited interracial marriage. The Supreme Court ruling would put an end to **race-based restrictions on marriage**. The case originated when Mildred Jeter and Richard Loving, an interracial Virginia couple that was married in Washington, DC due to the Virginia state law prohibiting interracial marriage, returned to Virginia and received charges of violating the interracial marriage ban. After pleading guilty, the couple was forced to move to DC to avoid a jail sentence, where they brought their case to the Supreme Court on the premise that their Fourteenth Amendment rights had been violated. The Supreme Court found that the Virginia law was unconstitutional and overturned the conviction that the couple had been charged with.

Jones v. Mayer

Jones v. Mayer was a 1968 Supreme Court case that ruled that Congress has the authority to **regulate the sale of private property** for the purpose of preventing racial discrimination. This United States Supreme Court ruling was based on a legal statute that stipulates that it is illegal in the United States to commit acts of racial discrimination, both privately and publicly when selling or renting property. The United States Supreme Court ruled that the congressional power to uphold the statute extends from the power of Congress to uphold the Thirteenth Amendment.

Roe v. Wade

Roe v. Wade was a controversial 1973 US Supreme Court case. The case originated in 1970 in Texas, which had an **anti-abortion law**. The plaintiff was an unmarried pregnant woman who was assigned the name "Jane Roe" to protect her identity. Texas anti-abortion law characterized the acts of having or attempting to perform an abortion as crimes, with the exception of cases in which an abortion could save the life of a mother. The lawsuit argued that the Texas law was unconstitutionally vague and was not consistent with the rights guaranteed by the First, Fourth, Fifth, Ninth, and Fourteenth Amendments. While the Texas court ruled in favor of Roe, it did not rule that Texas had to discontinue the enforcement of its anti-abortion law. Roe appealed to the Supreme Court in 1971, and the court's decision in 1973 struck down Texas's abortion laws. The case overturned most state laws prohibiting abortion. In 2022, the supreme court reversed its decision in Roe v Wade, finding no constitutional basis for requiring states to permit abortion, effectively returning the authority to the states to decide.

Regents of the University of California v. Bakke

Regents of the University of California v. Bakke was a 1978 Supreme Court case that banned **quota systems** in the college admissions process but ruled that programs providing **advantages to minorities** are constitutionally sound. The case originated when Allan Bakke, a white male who was a strong student, applied to the University of California at Davis Medical School and was rejected. The school had a program that reserved admissions spots for minority applicants; the program had grown along with the overall size of the school since its opening in 1968. Bakke complained to the school but was still not admitted, and he finally brought his case before the Superior Court of California. The California court ruled in favor of Bakke, who claimed that he had been discriminated against because of his race, and the school appealed to the US Supreme Court. The Supreme Court ruled that race could be used as one factor by discriminatory boards such as college admissions boards; however, quotas were ruled to be **discriminatory**.

Americans with Disabilities Act (ADA)

The ADA was passed by Congress in 1990. This act outlines the rights of individuals with disabilities in society in all ways besides education. It states that they should receive **nondiscriminatory treatment** in jobs, **access** to businesses and other stores, and other services. Due to this law all businesses must be wheelchair accessible, having a ramp that fits the standards of the law, and all doors and bathrooms within those businesses must be able to be used and maneuvered through by someone in a wheelchair. If these rules are not followed, businesses can be subject to large fines until these modifications have been complied with. The ADA also ensures fair treatment when applying for jobs to make sure that there is no unfair discrimination for any person with a disability who is applying to the job.

The Civil Rights Act of 1991

The Civil Rights Act of 1991 is a statute that was passed as a result of a number of Supreme Court decisions that restricted the rights of individuals who had sued their employers on the basis of discrimination. The passing of the **Civil Rights Act of 1991** was the first time since the Civil Rights Act of 1964 was passed that modifications were made to the rights granted under federal laws to individuals in cases involving **employment discrimination**. Specifically, the Civil Rights Act of 1991 granted the right to a trial by jury to individuals involved in cases of employment discrimination, and it also addressed for the first time the potential for emotional distress damages and limited the amount awarded by a jury in such cases.

Planned Parenthood v. Casey

Planned Parenthood of Southeastern Pennsylvania v. Casey was a 1992 Supreme Court case that challenged the constitutionality of Pennsylvania abortion laws. The case was brought before the US District Court for the Eastern District of Pennsylvania by abortion clinics and physicians to challenge four clauses of the **Pennsylvania Abortion Control Act of 1982** as unconstitutional under Roe v. Wade. The district court ruled that all of the clauses of the Pennsylvania act were unconstitutional. The case was then appealed to the Third Circuit Court of Appeals, which ruled to uphold all of the clauses except for one requiring notification of a husband prior to abortion. The case was then appealed to the Supreme Court, which ruled to uphold the constitutional right to have an abortion, thereby upholding Roe v. Wade.

Adarand Constructors, Inc. v. Peña

Adarand Constructors, Inc. v. Peña was a 1995 United States Supreme Court case in which the court ruled that any **racial classifications** that are instituted by representatives of federal, state, or local governments have to be reviewed and analyzed by a court. The court that reviews such racial classifications must abide by a policy of **strict scrutiny**. Strict scrutiny represents the highest standard of Supreme Court review. Racial classifications are deemed constitutional solely under circumstances in which they are being used as specific measures to advance critical and important governmental interests. The ruling of the Supreme Court in this case requiring strict scrutiny as a standard of review for racial classifications overturned the case of **Metro Broadcasting, Inc. v. FCC**, in which the Supreme Court established a two-level method of reviewing and analyzing racial classifications.

The Employment Non-Discrimination Act (ENDA) and the Equality Act

The Employment Non-Discrimination Act was a proposed United States federal law that was introduced various times before Congress but was never passed by both the House and the Senate. The **Employment Non-Discrimination Act** would ban employers from discriminating against their employees based on their **sexual orientation**. A number of states have already passed laws that ban discrimination based on sexual orientation, including California, Connecticut, Hawaii, Maryland, Massachusetts, Minnesota, Nevada, New Hampshire, New Jersey, New Mexico, New York, Rhode Island, Vermont, and Wisconsin. The ENDA has largely been encompassed by a broader resolution known as the Equality Act, which is a bill that would amend the Civil Rights Act of 1964 to further add gender identity and sexual orientation to the list of prohibited categories of discrimination for employment, public accomodations, the jury system, and housing. It has been met with opposition and has not yet been passed by both bodies of Congress.

Miranda v. Arizona

In 1966, the Supreme Court ruled that law enforcement must warn a person of their constitutional rights before interrogating them. If these rights—known as Miranda rights—are not explained to a person, that person's statements cannot be used as evidence against them at trial. The Supreme Court held that interrogating people without informing of them of their rights is in violation of their Constitutional rights.

In this case, Ernesto Miranda was arrested and charged with the kidnapping and rape of an 18-year-old woman. Miranda was not informed of his right to an attorney or to silence before or during the two-hour long interrogation he was subjected to by the police. The interrogation resulted in both oral and written confessions, which were both brought against Miranda in trial. They were initially accepted as evidence, resulting in Miranda being sentenced for 20-30 years in prison. The conviction was reversed after the Supreme Court's decision, though Miranda was later found guilty of the same crime in a later trial.

Grutter v. Bollinger

Grutter v. Bollinger was a 2003 Supreme Court case that upheld an **affirmative action policy** of the University of Michigan Law School admissions process. The case originated in 1996 when Barbara Grutter, a white in-state resident with a strong academic record, applied to the law school and was denied admission. In 1997, she filed a lawsuit claiming that her rejection was based on racial discrimination and violated her Fourteenth Amendment rights, as well as Title VI of the Civil Rights Act of 1964. The case was heard in 2001 in a US District Court, which ruled that the university's admissions policies were unconstitutional. In 2002, the case was appealed to the Sixth Circuit Court of Appeals, which overturned the lower court's decision. The case was then appealed to the US Supreme Court in 2003, which ruled that the school's affirmative action policy could remain in place, upholding the case of Regents of the University of California v. Bakke permitting race to be a factor in admissions but banning quotas.

Chapter Quiz

Ready to see how well you retained what you just read? Scan the QR code to go directly to the chapter quiz interface for this study guide. If you're using a computer, simply visit the online resources page at **mometrix.com/resources719/ssregushistgov** and click the Chapter Quizzes link.

Practice Test #1

Want to take this practice test in an online interactive format?
Check out the online resources page, which includes interactive practice questions and much more: **mometrix.com/resources719/ssregushistgov**

Use the excerpt and your knowledge of social studies to answer the following questions from the opening of the Declaration of Independence:

> "IN CONGRESS, July 4, 1776.
>
> The unanimous Declaration of the thirteen united States of America,
>
> When in the Course of human events, it becomes necessary for one people to dissolve the political bands which have connected them with another, and to assume among the powers of the earth, the separate and equal station to which the Laws of Nature and of Nature's God entitle them, a decent respect to the opinions of mankind requires that they should declare the causes which impel them to the separation."

1. Which of the following sentences BEST summarizes the meaning of the excerpt?

a. The thirteen colonies were planning to give separate but equal rights to African-American slaves.
b. The thirteen colonies had been attacked by British troops, and wanted to list their reasons for fighting back against England.
c. The thirteen colonies were forming their own government separate from the King of England, and they planned to outline the reasons for their revolution against England.
d. The thirteen colonies would form their own government separate from England, but they would list the laws of nature which kept them attached to England for some purposes.

2. What grassroots political movement, started by southern and western farmers, arose in the 1890s U.S. to fight banks, railroads, large corporations and other "elites"?

a. Entrepreneurship Movement
b. Farmers United
c. Populist Movement
d. Social Gospel Movement

3. Which characteristic has NOT yet been used to define a historical era in U.S. History?

a. A land form
b. Years of war
c. Years of social reforms
d. A time of economic growth or failure

4. Which momentous event related to the Spanish-America War occurred in 1898?

a. America gave financial support to Cuban nationalists' revolution against Spain.
b. Americans blamed Spain for the sinking of the *USS Maine*.
c. The Philippines declared independence from U.S. rule after Spain had transferred their rule of the Philippines to the U.S.
d. The U.S. withdrew from Cuba.

5. The 1887 General Allotment Act, also known as the Dawes Act, had a policy of giving private property ownership to Native Americans in order to divide the Native American reservations into individual "family farms." What was a practical result of this policy?

a. Many Native American tribes lost large portions of their reservations.
b. Many Native Americans became assimilated to the American culture of family farming.
c. The Nez Perce Conflict occurred between Nez Perce Native Americans and U.S. army forces.
d. American settlers moved to lands formerly owned by Native Americans and slaughtered most of the buffalo that Native Americans depended on for their livelihood.

6. In 1880, every state and territory in the U.S. had railway tracks. Which statement BEST describes an effect of railroad growth on the U.S. economy in the 1880s?

a. Railroad companies had to pay higher wages to employees
b. It provided better links between raw materials and markets
c. It increased competition between states and territories
d. It decreased taxes that railroad companies had to pay

Use the excerpt and your knowledge of social studies to answer the following question:

> U.S. Navy Captain Alfred Thayer Mahan wrote an essay in 1890 including this statement:
>
> "The interesting and significant feature of this changing attitude [in America] is the turning of the eyes outward, instead of inward only, to seek the welfare of the country."

7. In the above quote, what was Mahan correctly predicting would occur more often in the 1890s?

a. U.S. expansionism
b. U.S. western settlement
c. U.S. entry into World War I
d. U.S. census bureau increasing counts

Use the timeline and your knowledge of social studies to answer the following question:

Timeline of Events in Puerto Rico's History

1902 United States declares Puerto Rico a territory

1904 Unionist Party of Puerto Rico forms as political opposition against the colonial U.S. government

1914 Native Puerto Rican islanders' form a majority in the government's Executive Cabinet for this first time in the island's history as a U.S. territory

1917 President Wilson signs the Jones Act which made Puerto Rico an "organized but unincorporated" territory, gave the island more autonomy in their government, and gave U.S. citizen status to Puerto Ricans

8. Which conclusion is MOST true based on information in the above timeline?

a. Native Puerto Ricans had a majority in the island's government from the beginning of their time as a U.S. territory
b. Spanish was declared the official language of Puerto Rico, even though the island became a U.S. territory
c. Puerto Rico succumbed to U.S. expansionism but also advocated to get more rights for the island natives
d. Puerto Rico natives formed a violent revolution against U.S. colonialism

9. The first "May Day" celebration for the rights of working people occurred in the U.S. on May 1, 1886, with more than 300,000 workers across the country participating in a one-day strike. Which factor below BEST describes one cause of this historic event?

a. Government policies on Native Americans meant that this group was assimilating into groups of workers, but they were also causing agitation among workers.
b. By 1886, union membership had grown to a high point, such as with a group called Knights of Labor having a membership of one million workers.
c. A law passed in 1885 raising an income tax on working people had caused a lot of anger among average workers.
d. Immigrants from European countries brought the May Day tradition from their countries to U.S. workers.

10. Which of the following was one of the terms in the Treaty of Versailles at the end of World War I?

a. Germany had lands in Europe taken away but was able to keep their overseas colonies.
b. The German army was reduced but they were allowed to keep tanks.
c. Germany had to admit full responsibility for starting the war.
d. Germany was allowed to unite with Austria.

Use the excerpt and your knowledge of social studies to answer the following question:

From The Jungle, by Upton Sinclair, 1906

"The packers had secret mains, through which they stole billions of gallons of the city's water. The newspapers had been full of this scandal—once there had even been an investigation, and an actual uncovering of the pipes; but nobody had been punished, and the thing went right on. And then there was the condemned meat industry, with its endless horrors. The people of Chicago saw the government inspectors in Packingtown, and they all took that to mean that they were protected from diseased meat; they did not understand that these hundred and sixty-three inspectors had been appointed at the request of the packers, and that they were paid by the United States government to certify that all the diseased meat was kept in the state."

11. After President Theodore Roosevelt read "The Jungle," he ordered an investigation of the meat packing industry. What else MOST likely was a result of the book and the investigation?

a. Upton Sinclair ran a successful campaign to become the first Socialist congressional representative from New Jersey
b. Upton Sinclair published several other books that were just as commercially successful as "The Jungle" was
c. Theodore Roosevelt announced that he agreed with Upton Sinclair's political philosophy of socialism
d. Congress passed a "Pure Food and Drugs Act" and a "Meat Inspection Act" in 1906

Use the newspaper image and your knowledge of social studies to answer the following question:

THE AMERICAN ISSUE

U.S. IS VOTED DRY

36th STATE RATIFIES DRY AMENDMENT JAN. 16

Nebraska Noses Out Missouri for Honor of Completing Job of Writing Dry Act Into the Constitution; Wyoming, Wisconsin and Minnesota Right on Their Heels

JANUARY 16, 1919, MOMENTOUS DAY IN WORLD'S HISTORY

12. Which amendment is referenced in this newspaper headline?

a. 16th Amendment
b. 17th Amendment
c. 18th Amendment
d. 19th Amendment

13. Harry Laughlin, a scientist and eugenicist, testified in Congressional hearings on immigration policies in the early 1920s that immigrants from some European countries were biologically inferior to native-born white Americans. Laughlin claimed that immigrants had lower intelligence test scores and higher rates of criminal activity. What was one result of such eugenicist theories?

a. The Johnson Act was passed by Congress in 1924 to restrict annual immigration from certain regions of Europe
b. Congress passed an act in 1923 to increase the numbers of prisons in cities with high immigrant populations
c. The eugenics theories led believers in 1925 to form their own political party known as the Populists
d. Ellis Island closed in 1925 and no longer processed any immigrants into the U.S.

14. In 1918, Marcus Garvey started a newspaper in the U.S. called *The Negro World*, which promoted Garvey's philosophy of black pride, self-help, and economic independence for African Americans and Africans anywhere in the world. What other movement in the 1920s could be said to have been influenced by Marcus Garvey's ideas?

a. Accommodation
b. Black Panthers
c. Social Darwinism
d. Harlem Renaissance

Use the timeline and your knowledge of social studies to answer the following question:

Aggressions by Dictators in 1930s to early 1940s

1936 Italy (under Benito Mussolini) attacked and took over Ethiopia

1938 Germany (under dictator Adolf Hitler) took over Austria

1939 Hitler invaded Poland

15. Which event could be added to this timeline to show the final cause for Americans entering into World War II?

a. 1939 Japan entered an alliance with Germany and Italy
b. 1940 Germany invaded France
c. 1940 Germany invaded Denmark and Norway
d. 1941 Fascist government in Japan bombed Pearl Harbor

Use the excerpt and your knowledge of social studies to answer the following question:

> "Project TRINITY was the name given to the war-time effort [in the United States] to produce the first nuclear detonation. A plutonium-fueled implosion device was detonated on 16 July 1945 at the Alamogordo Bombing Range in south-central New Mexico."
>
> *-from Project Trinity 1945-1946, by Carl Maag and Steve Rohrer*

16. Why was Project Trinity a very important program for the U.S. during World War II?

a. The U.S. wanted to use nuclear energy to power their factories in helping the war effort.
b. Germany and Japan both had programs to build an atomic bomb, so the U.S. needed one first to win the war.
c. Italy and Germany both had plans to build an atomic bomb, so the U.S. needed to build one before their enemies did.
d. The U.S. wanted to use the threat of a nuclear bomb to put down any insurrections that might start in Japanese internment camps in New Mexico.

Use the list and your knowledge of social studies to answer the following question:

Around 160,000 Allied troops landed along a 50-mile stretch of French coastline to fight Nazi Germany.

More than 5,000 ships and 13,000 aircraft gave support for the Allied attack.

17. Which World War II battle does the above information describe?

a. D-day, the Normandy Invasion
b. Battle of the Bulge
c. Battle of Midway
d. Battle of Britain

Use the photograph and your knowledge of social studies to answer the following question:

Some victory gardeners displaying their vegetables 1942 or 1943

18. What was one main purpose of a Victory Garden in the U.S. during World War II?

a. To ensure that the domestic food supply was not being poisoned by foreign spies or infiltrators
b. To decrease demand on commercial vegetable growers, making more food available to soldiers
c. To provide more nutritious food for poor immigrant populations
d. To sell grown foods at markets and raise money for war bonds

Use the map and your knowledge of social studies to answer the following question:

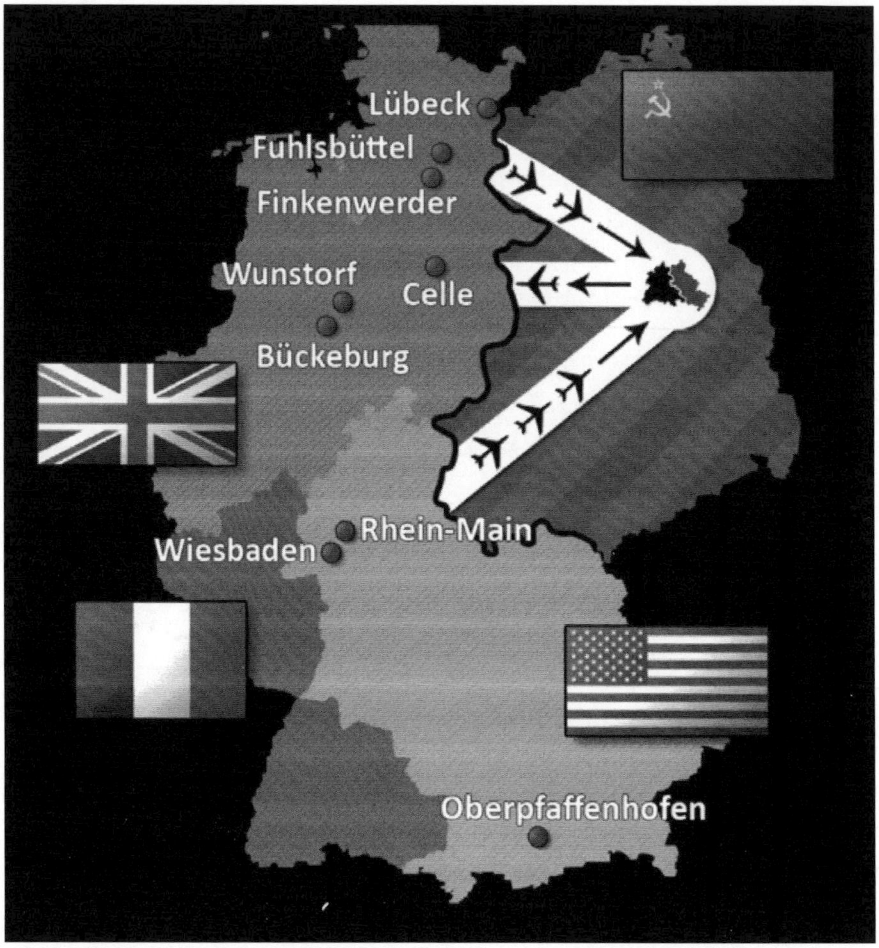

Post World War II Germany, around 1948-49, showing Germany divided into the American sector, British sector, French sector, and Russian sector. The capital city of Berlin was also divided into those four sectors after the war.

19. This map shows political divisions of Germany after World War II. What else does this map illustrate with the use of arrows?

a. The area designated as "free airspace" where travelers from the different sectors could travel in between East and West Germany
b. The "Berlin Bombing" routes used by Allied aircraft to bomb enemy targets in East Berlin that were under control of the U.S.S.R.
c. The "Berlin Airlift," the routes used by Allied aircraft to airlift supplies to West Berlin because the Soviet Union was imposing a blockade on supplies to West Berlin
d. The plans for moving Germany's defeated air force and airplanes in between new airports owned by Soviet, American, French, and British governments

Use the list and your knowledge of social studies to answer the following question:

- Communist North Korea invaded South Korea in 1950.
- President Truman worried that the Soviet Union and China planned to expand communism throughout Asia.
- The United Nations passed a resolution in 1950 urging United Nations member countries to give assistance to South Korea in their battle against North Korea.

20. What would be the BEST title for this list that summarizes what all of the items on the list have in common?

a. Reasons Why the Policy of Containment was Ineffective
b. Reasons for United States Involvement in the Korean War
c. Reasons for the Popularity of McCarthyism in the United States
d. Reasons Why the House Un-American Activities Committee Formed

21. In 1969, President Nixon made a speech about the Vietnam War and referred to a "silent majority" of Americans. Which Americans did he define as the "silent majority"?

a. Americans who were against the Vietnam War but were not actively protesting in the streets.
b. Americans who supported the Vietnam War but were not overly expressive about their opinions, unlike certain loud war protestors.
c. American troops who had returned from fighting in the Vietnam War in need of social services, even though they did not loudly demand such services.
d. American politicians who were quietly listening to opinions about the Vietnam War from their constituents before making any political decisions about the war.

Use the excerpt and your knowledge of social studies to answer the following question:

The Black Experience in America by Norman Coombs, 1972

"During Reconstruction blacks played a significant political role throughout the South. Besides voting in large numbers, they were elected to local, state, and federal offices. Between 1869 and 1901, two became U. S. Senators and twenty were members of the House of Representatives. Senators Revels and Bruce were elected from Mississippi. P. B. S. Pinchback was elected to the Senate from Louisiana, but he was not permitted to take his seat. He did serve as Lieutenant Governor of Louisiana, and, for three days, was Acting Governor."

22. Which amendment MOST made the above events possible?

a. 13th Amendment
b. 14th Amendment
c. 15th Amendment
d. 19th Amendment

Use the chart and your knowledge of social studies to answer the following question:

Chart—Percentage of African Americans in Certain Military Ranks, 1964-1966

Rank E-6 (Staff Sergeant or Petty Officer, First Class)

	1964	1965	1966
Army	13.9	15.5	18.1
Navy	4.7	5.0	5.6
Marine Corps	5.0	5.3	10.4

Source: Office, Deputy Assistant Secretary of Defense (Civil Rights)

23. In the early 1960s, President Kennedy became more committed to helping civil rights causes, including the cause of desegregation in the military. Based on this chart, what conclusion about African Americans in 1964-66 military ranks can be made?

a. African Americans started making up a larger percentage of Major or Lieutenant Commander Ranks in the Army, Navy, and Marines
b. African Americans started making up a larger percentage of Staff Sergeant or Petty Officer Ranks in the Army, Navy, and Marines
c. African Americans started making up a larger percentage of Staff Sergeant or Petty Officer Ranks in the Army and Marines, but not in the Navy.
d. The percentage of African-American Staff Sergeants or Petty Officers grew between 1954 and 1965, but then declined again between 1965 and 1966

24. Which part of the Iran-Contra affair (that took place under President Reagan in the 1980s) consisted of illegal activities?

a. The U.S. convinced other countries to sell weapons to Iran. The Contras inside the Nicaraguan government also sold weapons to Iran.
b. Iran was allowed to begin research into nuclear weapons. Contras fighting the government in Nicaragua were allowed to buy weapons from Iran.
c. Weapons were illegally sold to Iran by the U.S. government. Funds from the arms sales were illegally diverted to support the Contras, a group fighting the Nicaraguan government.
d. The U.S. sold weapons to the Contras, a group supporting the Nicaraguan government. Funds from the arms sales were illegally diverted to a group inside Iran fighting that government.

Use the excerpt and your knowledge of social studies to answer the following question:

"America is at war with a transnational terrorist movement fueled by a radical ideology of hatred, oppression, and murder. Our National Strategy for Combating Terrorism, first published in February 2003, recognizes that we are at war and that protecting and defending the Homeland, the American people, and their livelihoods remains our first and most solemn obligation."

From *National Strategy for Combating Terrorism*, Sept. 2006

25. What was another name for the "National Strategy for Combating Terrorism"?

a. Homeland Radicalism
b. Persian Gulf War
c. Terrorism Crisis
d. War on Terror

Use the excerpt and your knowledge of social studies to answer the following question:

> "There is a time to every purpose under the heaven--a time of war and a time of peace." So spoke one of Woodstock's most famous sons, the Reverend John Peter Gabriel Muhlenberg, in the Lutheran Church one Sunday morning after the Declaration of Independence had been issued. After delivering an inspired sermon taken from this text in which he reviewed his stand on liberty, he dramatically cast off his black pulpit robes and revealed to his astonished congregation his colonel's uniform of the Revolutionary army."

26. The excerpt describes two careers that John Peter Muhlenberg had before and during the Revolutionary War period. What were those two careers, and what third career did he have after the Revolutionary War?

a. Reverend, British Army Colonel, first Governor of Virginia
b. Speaker, British Army soldier, first Governor of Connecticut
c. Reverend, Continental Army Colonel, member of the first U.S. Congress
d. Writer, signer of the Declaration of Independence, Continental Army soldier

27. What was the primary purpose of the Chinese Exclusion Act passed by the U.S. Congress in 1882?

a. To ban Chinese from immigrating to the U.S.
b. To exclude Chinese Americans from joining unions in the U.S.
c. To ban Chinese Americans from working on railroads in the U.S.
d. To exclude Chinese from claiming settlement lands in the western U.S.

Use the photo and your knowledge of social studies to answer the following question:

Alvan Macauley (left), President of the Packard Motor Car Co. and Col. Charles A. Lindbergh with the original Packard diesel-powered Stinson "Detroiter" in the background, 1929. (Smithsonian photo A48319D.)

28. Besides flying some of the original diesel-powered airplanes, what was another notable contribution of Colonel Charles A. Lindbergh to 1920s U.S. history?

a. He made the first solo nonstop flight across the Atlantic Ocean in 1927.
b. He made the first solo nonstop flight across the Pacific Ocean in 1928.
c. He trained Amelia Earhart, the first female solo pilot, in piloting skills.
d. After Lindbergh's son was kidnapped, Congress passed the "Lindbergh Law," which made kidnapping a federal offense if a child was taken across state lines.

Use the chart and your knowledge of social studies to answer the following question:

The only unbroken code in modern military history used Native-American words for military words, but words were not direct translations. The Native-American words were for something similar to the military term being described, for example:

Native American word	Translation	Code for
chay-da-gahi	Tortoise	Tank
gini	Chicken hawk (a bird that dives on its prey).	Dive bomber
ne-he-mah	Our mother	America

29. What was the name of the U.S. Marines group that used this code, and in which war was it used to communicate securely and save lives?

a. Navajo Code Talkers, World War I
b. Navajo Code Talkers, World War II
c. Sioux Secret Coders, World War I
d. Sioux Secret Coders, World War II

30. Although pressured to take military action by some advisors, President John F. Kennedy prevailed in his 1962 strategy of getting the Soviet Union to end the construction of bases for nuclear missiles on an island in return for a U.S. promise to not invade that island. Those "13 Days in October" are more famously known by what name?

a. Dominican Republic Nuclear Danger
b. Dominican Republic at the Brink
c. Cuban Communist Crisis
d. Cuban Missile Crisis

Use the excerpt and your knowledge of social studies to answer the following question:

> "The animals which are found west of the Missouri River, especially in the Rocky Mountains, and far beyond them, are the buffalo, elk, deer, cimarron bear, mountain sheep, antelope, coyote, prairie-dog, etc.
>
> The buffalo, which affords good beef to the Indian hunters, and has fed many thousand toilers over the plains to Salt Lake and California, is mainly known to boys in the comfortable buffalo robes, which everyone knows the use of in sleigh-riding. But to us officers and soldiers on the plains they are life-preservers almost, in our sleeping out nights on the ground, far away from home and good beds and blankets."
>
> From *Three Years on the Plains* by Edmund B. Tuttle, 1870

31. Based on this excerpt, which statement would be MOST likely true about whites' settlement of the Great Plains in the late 1800s?

a. Like the Native Americans of the Great Plains, white settlers also came to rely on buffalo for food and for providing warm robes on cold nights
b. In the Great Plains there were many animals that could provide food for new white settlers, but there were not any dangerous animals
c. The white settlers came to rely on buffalo for providing food and on elk and deer for use in sleigh-riding
d. The white settlers in the Great Plains came to rely on buffalo for food, but not for any other purpose

Use the map and your knowledge of social studies to answer the following question:

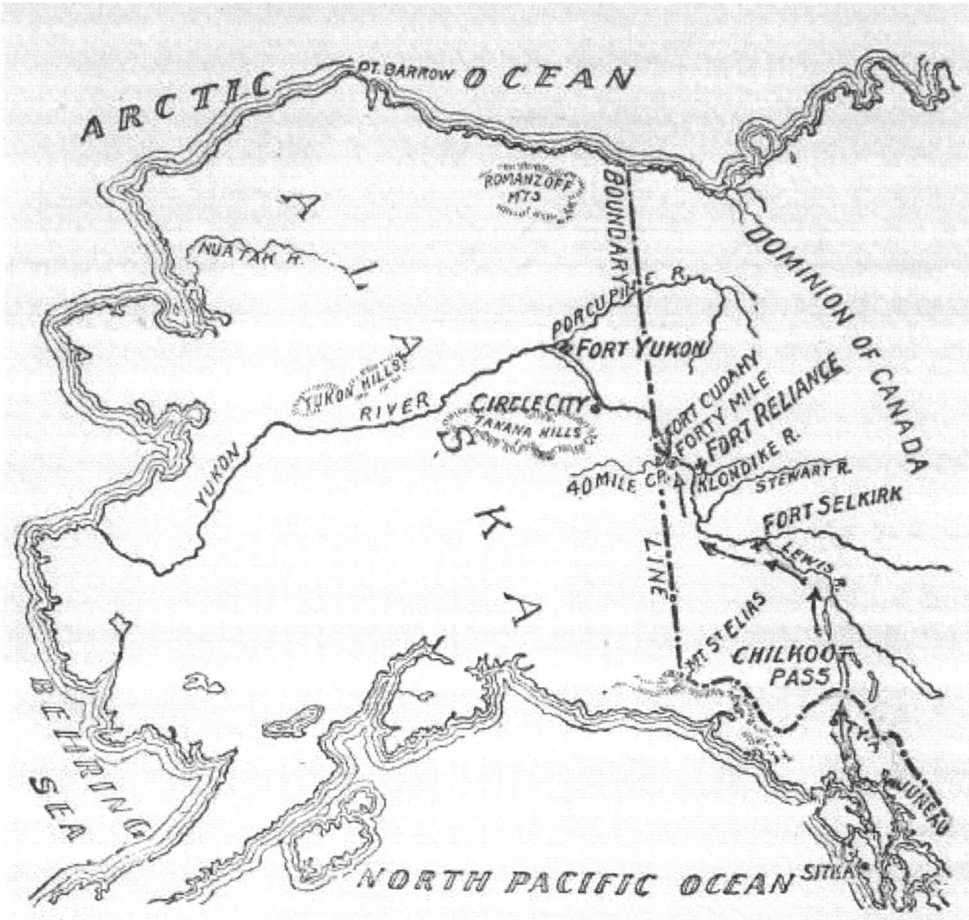

MAP OF THE YUKON GOLD DIGGINGS

32. In the 1890s, gold was discovered in the Klondike area of Alaska, and a rush of settlers came to the area. Based on the map, which of the following is MOST likely the correct order and route of how miners traveled in the area?

a. Miners buy supplies in Juneau, pack their loads and hike through Chilkoot Pass, take boats down Lewis River to the Klondike River, hike from the river to the Yukon Hills
b. Miners buy supplies in Juneau, ride on steamboats to Ty-a, pack their loads and hike through Chilkoot Pass, take boats down Lewis River to the Klondike River
c. Miners hike through the Chilkoot Pass, take boats down Lewis River to the Klondike River, buy supplies at the town of Forty Mile, pack their loads and hike forty miles into Canada
d. Miners hike through the Chilkoot Pass, take boats down Lewis River to the Klondike River, walk along that river bank to Circle City, buy supplies at Circle City

Use the excerpt and your knowledge of social studies to answer the following question:

> "At Panama earthquakes are few and unimportant, while the Nicaraguan route passes over a well-known coastal weakness. Only five disturbances of any sort were recorded at Panama, all very slight, while similar official records at San Jose de Costa Rica, near the route of the Nicaragua Canal, show for the same period fifty shocks, a number of which were severe."

> And later he continued: "The situation being, then, that the danger from volcanoes at Panama is nothing, and that from earthquakes practically nothing, while at Nicaragua the canal would be situated in one of the most dangerous regions of the world from both these causes, the question should be considered settled."

33. Based on this excerpt, which statement would be MOST likely true about the Panama Canal?

a. When considering where to build a canal in Central America, factors such as earthquakes and volcanoes needed to be taken into consideration.
b. It was risky to build a canal in Panama because of possible volcanoes there, but the risk of earthquakes in Nicaragua was greater.
c. There were never any volcanoes or earthquakes in Nicaragua, so there was no danger to building a canal there.
d. There were never any volcanoes or earthquakes in Panama, so there was no danger to building a canal there.

Use the excerpt and your knowledge of social studies to answer the following question:

> "Some say that they left the South on account of injustice in the courts, unrest, lack of privileges, denial of the right to vote, bad treatment, oppression, segregation or lynching. Others say that they left to find employment, to secure better wages, better school facilities, and better opportunities to toil upward."

34. What would be the BEST summary of this excerpt?

a. Causes of Confederate Soldiers Abandoning the South
b. Effects of Migration from the Rust Belt to the Sun Belt
c. Causes of the Great Migration
d. Effects of Western Expansion

35. A study in 1998 found that new immigrants to the U.S. tended to settle in the "port-of-entry" states where they first entered the United States. How would this fact MOST likely affect demographics within the U.S.?

a. There would be a high number of immigrants settling in states such as California, New York, and Texas
b. There would be a high number of immigrants settling in states such as Colorado, Utah, and Nebraska
c. Native-born Americans would leave the states where new immigrants were settling
d. It would have no effect on demographics within the United States

36. Tin Pan Alley referred to the location in New York City of popular music publishers, and also to the kind of music being produced there in the 1890s and early 20th century. What were one negative impact and one positive impact of Tin Pan Alley?

a. *Positive:* Tin Pan Alley was the birthplace of American popular music and created the ASCAP (American Society of Composers, Authors, and Publishers).
   Negative: ASCAP was a predominantly white group for many years until the popularity of music by African Americans arose in the late 1920s.
b. *Positive*: Tin Pan Alley sold millions of copies of sheet music.
   Negative: The Tin Pan Alley location still has many music publishers but has become a high-crime area.
c. *Positive:* Tin Pan Alley gave a lot of jobs to new immigrants.
   Negative: All the money earned went to publishing companies, while composers stayed poor.
d. *Positive*: Sheet music could now be sold to the public, instead of just to professional performers.
   Negative: Tin Pan Alley did not hire any immigrants.

Use the list and your knowledge of social studies to answer the following question:

Disneyland
Hollywood movies
McDonald's restaurants
Pop music
Television shows

37. Which heading would BEST describe something that the items on this list have in common?

a. Things That Began in the 1920s
b. Things That Began in the 1930s
c. Things That Are Headquartered in California
d. American Pop Culture Influences on the World

Use the illustration and your knowledge of social studies to answer the following question:

Group of Converted Indians with their Pastor

38. This illustration BEST gives an example of which historical process?

a. Migration of Native Americans to Reservations
b. Movement to Assimilate Native Americans into American Culture
c. Native American Battles with White Settlers
d. Evangelicals Within the Native American Community

Use the excerpt and your knowledge of social studies to answer the following question:

> *A famous woman social worker wrote this in her book about her work in 1910:*
>
> "In spite of these flourishing clubs for children early established at Hull-House, and the fact that our first organized undertaking was a kindergarten, we were very insistent that the Settlement should not be primarily for the children, and that it was absurd to suppose that grown people would not respond to opportunities for education and social life."

39. Which famous woman did social work at Hull House in Chicago in the early 1900s and wrote that excerpt?

a. Susan B. Anthony
b. Jane Addams
c. Dr. Aletta Jacobs
d. Frances Willard

40. Which woman won an Outstanding Labor Leader Award for her lifetime work with Cesar Chavez on behalf of migrant farm workers in the U.S.?

a. Isabelle Allende
b. Gloria Anzaldua
c. Dolores Huerta
d. Sonia Sotomayor

41. The Great Seal of the United States that was first used in 1782 included the motto *E Pluribus Unum*. The same motto appeared on federal coins in 1795. What is the meaning of this motto?

a. In God We Trust
b. In Union We Trust
c. Out of Many, One
d. The Many are United

42. In 1997, President Clinton presented the Congressional Medal of Honor to Vernon J. Baker, a 78-year-old African American, for his courage and leadership in attacks on the enemy in Italy during a previous war. Racial prejudice during the time of this war had prevented Baker from receiving the award previously. In which war did Vernon Baker bravely fight?

a. World War I
b. World War II
c. Korean War
d. Vietnam War

43. President Franklin Roosevelt's New Deal legislation included retirement income for elderly, farm subsidies, insurance for bank deposits, public works projects, benefits for the unemployed, and more. What kind of historic change did such programs represent?

a. It was the first time that federal legislation affected farmers
b. It was the first time that the Supreme Court had the final authority to approve legislation
c. The programs gave state and federal governments increased power to affect the economy
d. The programs gave more power to state governments but took away power from the federal government.

44. The Ethics in Government Act of 1978 required elected public officials to make public some of their financial information. What could be considered a source of public demand for increased ethics in government at that time period?

a. The Watergate Scandal of the early 1970s had eroded some public trust in government officials.
b. The Teapot Dome Scandal of the late 1960s had eroded some public trust in government officials.
c. Newspapers had been making up stories in the early 1970s about public officials misusing government money.
d. Gerald Ford was not considered an ethical president, which was also the main reason he did not get re-elected to a second term.

45. Providing increased border patrols at the U.S.-Canada border was a provision of which legislation?

a. USA PATRIOT Act of 2001
b. Trade Act of 2002
c. Protection of Lawful Commerce in Arms Act of 2005
d. Secure Fence Act of 2006

46. Which statement below could be considered an advantage of the United States participating in the United Nations organization?

a. The United Nations does not involve itself in deadly conflicts or civil wars.
b. The United Nations has different foreign policy objectives than the United States has.
c. The United Nations has been a leader in helping to end the humanitarian and military crisis in Darfur.
d. The United Nations does not deal with relief for victims of natural disasters, thereby saving money for the United States.

47. In *Bush v. Gore*, the Supreme Court ruled 5-4 that a recount in that year's presidential election must take place by midnight of December 12th, 2000. The ruling came hours before the deadline, making it too late for a recount to actually occur. What is the BEST way to describe the historical aspect of this Supreme Court case?

a. This case caused states to make drastic changes in the ways that they supervised recounts in federal elections.
b. This case made history as the first time that a U.S. President had his name and cause appear in a Supreme Court case.
c. This case showed for the first time that presidential candidates needed to hire lawyers even before their campaigns started.
d. This case marked the first time that the judicial branch of government involved itself in a federal election, and critics said that the Supreme Court rather than the electorate had determined the winner of a presidential election.

48. In 1954, the Supreme Court's *Brown v. Board of Education* decision declared that school segregation and the "separate but equal" doctrine was unconstitutional. What happened afterward in southern states that same year?

a. Southern states immediately started planning how to desegregate their schools.
b. The Cold War started and everyone ignored the school desegregation movement for a few years.
c. The President immediately got involved in helping to desegregate schools in southern states, and he called in National Guard troops to assist.
d. Southern opponents of segregation used intimidation and violence against desegregation proponents, and many southern school districts avoided compliance with the new law.

49. In 1973's *White v. Regester* Supreme Court case, the court ruled that Texas county, city council, and school board districts should have elections so that members would be voted in from individual electoral districts. What kind of system did Texas have before this Supreme Court decision?

a. A vote by mail system that was full of fraud problems.
b. A voting system that allowed too many "write-in" candidates.
c. A poll tax that discouraged voters from poor districts from voting.
d. An "at large" voting system that had weakened minority voting power.

Use the excerpt and your knowledge of social studies to answer the following question:

> "Mr. Rockefeller wished me to join his board and this I did. Cooperation was soon found to be much to our mutual advantage, and we now work in unison."

50. Along with John D. Rockefeller, the industrialist who wrote the above quote in his autobiography was also one of the founders of corporate philanthropy in the 20th century. He donated to libraries, schools, universities, and former employees. Who was this wealthy industrialist?

a. Henry Ward Beecher
b. Andrew Carnegie
c. Elbert H. Gary
d. John Stuart Mill

Answer Key and Explanations for Test #1

1. C: It best summarizes the excerpt and shows knowledge of what else is outlined in the Declaration of Independence (grievances against England and reasons for declaring independence). Choice B would be a good guess, but the Declaration was written not because of attacks by British troops, but more because of rebellions by colonists. A student may pick choice A if they focus on the "separate but equal" clause in the excerpt, but the provision of "separate but equal" policies for African-American slaves came much later in U.S. history. A student might pick choice D if focused on the "Laws of Nature" phrase in the excerpt, but the colonists did not list such laws still connecting them to England in the Declaration.

2. C: The Populist movement arose in the U.S. in the 1890s as a grassroots political movement started by southern and western farmers to fight banks, railroads, large corporations and other "elites." "Farmers United" sounds like it could be a correct choice, given the involvement of farmers, but it is incorrect. Choice A and D are also incorrect, although the "Social Gospel" movement was active around the same time period. Entrepreneurship was also on the rise during that time period.

3. A: There has not yet been an era in U.S. History defined by a land form (for example, something like a "Rocky Mountain Era"). There was a Gold Rush era but that was not named specifically for a land form. So A is the BEST choice. There have been eras defined by wars (Civil War Era), economic growth or failure (Roaring Twenties, Great Depression), and by social reforms (Progressive Era).

4. B: The sinking of the USS Maine happened in 1898, and the fact that America blamed Spain was a major cause of the U.S. and Spain declaring war on each other in 1898. All the other events listed did not happen in 1898, so even though they are related to the Spanish-American War, they would not be the correct answer. Choice A happened in 1895, choice C occurred in 1899, and choice D happened in 1902.

5. A: Choice D sounds like a good option, because this is something that did happen, but it happened before the Dawes Act. The Nez Perce conflict of 1877 also occurred before the Dawes Act, so choice C is incorrect. Choice B was the hope of Dawes and other American politicians who planned the act in order to try to help "assimilate" Native Americans, but that was not the practical result as much as choice A, the taking over of reservation lands away from Native Americans.

6. B: Railroads did not have to pay higher wages to employees until after employees started unionizing in later years. For example, in the 1880s, they were still paying low wages to Chinese railway laborers. Choice B is the best answer: raw materials and markets were better connected for the distribution of economic products. Railroad companies probably did not see a big decrease in paying taxes, and probably had to pay more taxes to the various local governments where their tracks now ran through. States and territories became better connected by railroads, so "increased competition" would not be the best answer, either.

7. A: Mahan was correctly predicting that U.S. expansionism would increase in the 1890s as Americans increasingly turned their interests "outward," and not just inward to their own country. The country's entry into WWI would not come until the early 1900s, so that answer is incorrect. Western expansion mostly occurred before the 1890s and would still be looking "inward" at their own country, even though looking to expand settlements. Census bureau counts did increase in the 1890s, but that again is concerned with the U.S. looking "inward," examining their own population, rather than looking outward to expand into other countries.

8. C: The timeline facts show that Puerto Rico did succumb to U.S. expansionism by becoming a territory, but also that native islanders fought for more political rights. There was no major violent revolution against the U.S. in those years, and no minor ones are mentioned in the timeline, so that conclusion cannot be made. Spanish was not made the official language; English and Spanish were "co-official" for a time, and then English was made official in 1917. Also, languages are not mentioned in the timeline facts. Native Puerto Ricans did not have a majority in the island's government from the beginning of their time as a U.S. territory; that did not occur until 1914 (according to the timeline facts).

9. B: It is the only answer that relates to the growth of union membership in the late 1800s, and how this had a causal relationship to the first U.S. May Day celebration in 1886 of a massive one day strike. The other statements are all false. Choice D might be a good guess due to immigration at the time, but it is not the BEST choice listed for a cause of May Day

10. C: According to the Treaty of Versailles, Germany had to admit full responsibility for the war. Germany was forbidden to unite with Austria in the Treaty. The country also had lands in both Europe AND colonial lands taken away. They had to reduce their army number of soldiers and were not allowed to keep tanks anymore. So the other choices are all incorrect.

11. D: Congress did pass a Pure Food and Drugs Act and a Meat Inspection Act in 1906 after the president ordered an investigation of the meat packing industry due to being concerned with passages from "The Jungle" by Upton Sinclair (like the passage excerpt quoted). Sinclair did subsequently write other books, but they were not as commercially successful as "The Jungle," and nothing in the excerpt or question stem could support that statement, so it is not a good answer choice. Sinclair did run a campaign to become the first congressional representative from New Jersey to be a member of the Socialist Party, but he did not win. Roosevelt did not agree with Sinclair's socialist politics. Those answers should be eliminated by the student based on their general knowledge of social studies and that time period.

12. C: While the 16th, 17th, and 19th Amendments were in a similar time period as the 18th Amendment, the specific year 1919 and the reference to "being voted dry" are clues to a student who has some historical knowledge that this headline refers to the 18th Amendment. The 18th Amendment is the one prohibiting alcohol, thus the reference to becoming "dry."

13. A: It shows an effect caused by eugenics theories, which was a law restricting immigrants in 1924. But Ellis Island did not close completely until 1954 (later becoming a historic site and national park). The Populist political party was formed in the 1890s, so that answer is incorrect. Choice B sounds like it could be a result of eugenics theories but it is actually a made-up fact.

14. D: The 1920s Harlem Renaissance has been said by history professors to have been influenced by Marcus Garvey's movement of promoting black pride and black self-reliance. The Black Panthers were probably influenced by Garvey's ideas, but their movement did not begin until later in U.S. history. Accommodation was a movement promoted by leaders such as Booker T. Washington, around the same time as Garvey, but with somewhat opposite ideals from Garvey's promotion of economic independence. (Accommodation would be to interact economically with whites but accommodate to their separate but equal segregation rules.) Social Darwinism was a movement in the 1920s that could not be said to be influenced by Marcus Garvey, because most social Darwinists favored white races.

15. D: The Japanese attack on Pearl Harbor was the turning point which caused the U.S. to enter into World War II, even though the other events were all alarming to the U.S. and caused them to give financial assistance to the Allies before officially entering the war on the Allies' side. A student might guess that the alliance between Japan, Germany, and Italy was the turning point because it involves Japan becoming an Axis power, but it was the actual attack on Pearl Harbor which led to America entering the war.

16. B: Germany and Japan both had scientists working on nuclear bombs, and one of Project Trinity's most important goals was to make sure that the U.S. developed a bomb first and could thereby win the war through superior technology. Italy was not yet working on atomic bombs. A student might pick choice D because the excerpt mentions New Mexico and potential Japanese enemies, but that is incorrect. Choice A is also incorrect as the development of nuclear energy was not the goal of Project Trinity.

17. A: The "French coastline" is a clue that the Normandy Invasion is the correct answer, although a student may think "Bulge" or "Midway" is located in France. The high number of troops, ships, and aircraft is another clue that the facts describe D-Day. But a student not familiar with all of the other battles in World War II may pick one of the incorrect answers.

18. B: A main purpose of Victory Gardens was to decrease demand on commercial vegetable growers, thereby making more food available to soldiers. There were other purposes, such as providing nutritious foods to all people (not just poor immigrants) on the home front and boosting morale at home, but those were secondary and are not listed as answer choices. The other three answer choices listed are all incorrect.

19. C: The map's arrows show the routes the Berlin Airlift used to supply West Berlin with food supplies during a Soviet blockade. It does not show a bombing route, a route for moving captured German airplanes, or a route for tourists.

20. B: While all the titles have a connection of some kind to at least one or two items on the given list, choice B provides the BEST title for the list to show what all the items have in common: reasons for U.S. involvement in the Korean War. The policy of containment may have been partially effective, because Korea was only one country falling to communism. The United Nations item would probably not fall under a title about containment, McCarthyism, or the HUAC committee, because those were all more internal to the U.S. only. The U.N. was encouraging nations to get involved in the Korean War, so it fits under that title.

21. B: When Nixon referred to a "silent majority," he meant Americans who supported the Vietnam War but were not overly expressive about their opinions, unlike certain loud war protestors. The other options all relate to Americans and their relations to or opinions about the Vietnam War, but none of those are correct answers for the meaning of a "silent majority."

22. C: While the 13th and 14th Amendments granted important freedom from slavery and citizenship to African Americans, it was the 15th Amendment, a voting rights amendment, which made it possible for African Americans to elect each other as representatives by voting in large numbers. The 19th Amendment was also a voting rights amendment, but for women, and after the time period described in the excerpt.

23. B: This item tests the student's knowledge of armed forces desegregation AND the student's ability to read a chart. Reading the chart correctly and knowing general civil rights history will tell the student that choice B is correct. African Americans started making up a larger percentage of Staff Sergeant or Petty Officer Ranks in the Army, Navy, and Marines. If the student reads the type of officer rank incorrectly on the chart, he or she might pick choice A. The percentage of African-American staff sergeants and petty officers in the Navy did not increase as much as in the Army or

Marines, so a student might pick C, but there was still a slight increase, making choice C incorrect. Choice D is incorrect if the student understands the "years" columns in the charts.

24. C: It is the only choice that states what constituted illegal activities because they violated an arms embargo that was in place against Iran, and was an illegal diversion of funds. Weapons were illegally sold to Iran by the U.S. government. Funds from the arms sales were illegally diverted to support the Contras, a group fighting the Nicaraguan government. The other answer choices offer incorrect variations on these statements, or confuse the fact that Contras were against and not inside the Nicaraguan government.

25. D: The "War on Terror" is the correct terminology. "Homeland Radicalism" takes some words from the excerpt but does not describe how the U.S. was combating terrorism. The Persian Gulf War may have been one part of the War on Terror, but it does not include homeland security measures. The phrase "Terrorism Crisis" may have been used by the media or government at some point, but not as often as "War on Terror."

26. C: The excerpt gives information that Muhlenberg was a reverend and then a colonel in the Continental Army (as shown by his revealing of a Revolutionary colonel's uniform). The third correct choice is that he was one of the members of the first U.S. Congress, which the student should know from general social studies knowledge (as it is not in the excerpt). Or at least the student could use process of elimination to eliminate some of the other incorrect answers that claim he was first Governor of Connecticut or Virginia, a signer of the Declaration of Independence, or a British Army member.

27. A: The Chinese Exclusion Act of 1882 was passed for the purpose of banning Chinese immigrants from the United States. Students with knowledge of social issues affecting immigrants during that time period will know this answer. Choices C and D (prohibiting Chinese Americans from working on railroads or settling in the west) were probably secondary purposes of the act, but were not written into the legislation as choice A was.

28. A: Choices C and D are good guesses, because Amelia Earhart was the first female solo pilot, but Lindbergh did not train her. His son was kidnapped and it did lead to the law passed by Congress, but not until the mid-late 1930s. He was also not the first solo pilot across the Pacific in the 1920s. Choice A is correct: He was the first solo pilot to fly nonstop across the Atlantic Ocean in 1927.

29. B: The Navajo Code Talkers were the U.S. Marines group in World War II that used this code to save lives. The other choices all sound like reasonable alternatives, because tanks and dive bombers were used in World War I and II, and Sioux and Navajo were both American-Indian tribes at the time. Also, the term "code" appears in all four answer choices. But a student with general social studies knowledge at this grade level should know that B is the correct answer.

30. D: The Cuban Missile Crisis is the more famous name for the "13 Days in October" in which President John F. Kennedy played an important role. It is also sometimes called "World at the Brink," which may cause students to incorrectly choose answer B. It was a crisis involving fears of communism, which could lead students to incorrectly pick choice C. There was nuclear danger, and the Dominican Republic is another island in the Caribbean near the coast of America, which could lead students to incorrectly pick choice A. Their general knowledge of social studies at this grade level should lead to the correct choice of D.

31. A: Like the Native Americans of the Great Plains, white settlers also came to rely on buffalo for food and for providing warm robes on cold nights. The student needs to read the excerpt closely to understand that there were other uses for buffalo besides just food. A student who does not read the excerpt closely might pick choice C if he or she associated deer and elk with sleigh-riding, as many people do. A student might pick choice B if he or she considers that none of the animals listed are dangerous, though that could be a misreading because coyote, bear, and sometimes even buffalo and elk could be dangerous to settlers.

32. B: While it might be easier to buy supplies after the long hike through Chilkoot Pass, the fact was that miners would have to buy their supplies in the biggest city, Juneau, before making the rest of the trip. Also, some choices can be eliminated based on the fact that there does not seem to be a lot happening on the map at Yukon Hills or 40 miles into the Dominion of Canada. So choice B is the correct answer, which students can determine from the map, the arrows on the map, the collection of mining camps around the Klondike River, and their general knowledge of social studies: miners buy supplies in Juneau, steamboats carry them from Juneau to Ty-a, they pack their loads and hike through Chilkoot Pass, and they take boats down Lewis River to the Klondike River.

33. A: Choice D sounds possibly correct because the Senator is concluding that Panama is a superior location for a canal, but he notes that there actually were a few earthquakes in Panama, so it can't be said that there were **never** earthquakes in Panama. Choice A is correct that earthquake and volcano dangers to canals had to be considered when picking a location for a canal. Panama was chosen over Nicaragua because it had less earthquake risk and no volcano risk.

34. C: The excerpt gives a summary of Causes of the Great Migration. A student should know from general social studies knowledge that the Great Migration refers to movements of African Americans from southern states to states in the Northern, Western, and Midwestern United States. The excerpt gives the reasons why African Americans would make such a move. A student might pick answer A because of mention of the South (if not reading closely), or might pick the other choices for mention of migration or expansion, but only C is correct.

35. A: The fact that immigrants tended in the 1990s to settle in port-of-entry states means that, for U.S. demographics, there would be a high number of immigrants settling in states such as California, New York, and Texas. Colorado, Utah, and Nebraska are not typical port-of-entry states (even though they do have airports). The fact given does not provide any implication that native-born Americans would flee from states where new immigrants are settling. However, there is also no reason to think that there would be zero demographic effect from an influx of new immigrants, making choices C and D incorrect.

36. A: A positive impact of Tin Pan Alley was that it was the birthplace of American popular music and created the ASCAP (American Society of Composers, Authors, and Publishers). A negative about Tin Pan Alley and ASCAP was that it was a predominantly white group for many years until the late 1920s, when the popularity of blues and jazz music by African-American musicians gained them admittance into the ASCAP. For all the other choices, the positive impact listed is correct. But the negative impacts listed are all incorrect, thus making those choices all incorrect. Composers did become rich from Tin Pan Alley; the location is no longer a hub of music publishing companies today as it once was; and they did give jobs to many new immigrants, especially Jewish and Russian immigrants in NYC.

37. D: All of the items on the list represent American Pop Culture Influences on the World. Many of the list items do have headquarters in California, but McDonald's has its headquarters in Illinois. Some of the things began in the 1920s or 30s, but not all of them, so those answer choices would also be incorrect.

38. B: The illustration best shows an example of the Americanization Movement to Assimilate Native Americans into American Culture. There may have been a battle between Native Americans and white settlers before or after this illustration, but that is not shown in the picture. Native Americans did not tend to be evangelicals; rather, the white settlers were evangelical about converting Native Americans to their religion. The picture also does not detail the move of Native Americans to reservations, although that also could have become before or after the illustration shown.

39. B: Based on the fact that the excerpt mentions Hull House, and information is given that the woman was a famous social worker in Chicago in the early 1900s, the student should be able to figure out that Jane Addams is the correct answer. Dr. Jacobs was a Dutch suffragette leader who invited Addams to some international projects with her. Susan B. Anthony was also a suffragette, but in the U.S. and around the same time period as Addams. Frances Willard was a social reformer whose work was all done in the 1800s.

40. C: Dolores Huerta won the Outstanding Labor Leader Award from the state of California in 1984 recognizing her lifetime of work with Cesar Chavez on behalf of migrant farm workers. Gloria Anzaldua was a poet and cultural critic. Isabel Allende is a fiction writer from Chile. Sonia Sotomayor is a Supreme Court Justice.

41. C: The correct translation of *E Pluribus Unum* is "Out of Many, One." "In God We Trust" was adopted as the official motto of the U.S. later in history. "In Union We Trust" might be a good guess because "Unum" sounds like it could be a Latin version of "Union." "The many are united" also sounds like a plausible translation for *E Pluribus Unum*, even though it is actually incorrect.

42. B: The fact that Baker fought in Italy is a clue that either WWI or WWII is the correct answer, and that both the Korean War and Vietnam War would be incorrect, even though there was still some racial prejudice during the times of those wars. The fact that President Clinton presented Baker with the award gives a clue that it must have been for fighting during WWII, as Baker would probably not have been old enough to fight in WWI and still be alive under President Clinton's years. In fact, a student could deduce that, if Baker was 78 years old in 1997 that would mean he was born in 1919, which was after WWI. Also, general social studies knowledge suggests that students know who Vernon J. Baker is for this grade level.

43. C: The New Deal programs gave state and federal governments increased power to affect the economy. They did not take power away from the federal government. The programs did not need Supreme Court approval to be passed, because Congress passed the New Deal. And it was also not the first time that legislation affected farmers, because there was a Federal Farm Loan act in 1916, and other laws before the mid-1930s that probably affected farmers.

44. A: The Ethics in Government Act of 1978 was enacted after the Watergate Scandal of the early 1970s had eroded some public trust in government officials. The Teapot Dome Scandal occurred much earlier in the century, not in the 1960s. Newspapers were also not making up stories about unethical government officials, but they were reporting on Watergate. It is true that Gerald Ford did not get re-elected, partly because he was unpopular for pardoning Nixon, but not because he was considered unethical. Ford was not the impetus for the Ethics Act.

45. A: Providing increased border controls on the Canada-U.S. border was part of the USA PATRIOT Act of 2001 and affected the private and public sectors of people traveling between those two countries. The other choices listed all sound like they could be related to interactions between the U.S. and Canada. For example, lawful commerce in arms could relate to guns sold between countries, but it was for guns within the United States. A Trade Act might apply to U.S.-Canada trade, but not to border patrols. The "Fence" Act applied to the Mexico-U.S. border, not the Canada-U.S. border.

46. C: The U.N. has been a leader in helping end the crisis in Darfur, which helps the U.S. and its international image when it participates in the U.N. The other choices are all false statements. The U.N. does get involved in deadly conflicts, civil wars, and aid for victims of natural disasters. The U.N. also generally does have the same foreign policy objectives as the U.S.

47. D: This case marked the first time that the judicial branch of government involved itself in a federal election, and critics said that the Supreme Court rather than the electorate had determined the winner of a presidential election. However, it was later confirmed that Bush had fairly won the state of Florida and the election. There may have been some changes in the way states did recounts, but that is not the BEST description of the historical importance of the case. Choice B is incorrect because there had been other Supreme Court cases with president's names in them, such as *U.S. v. Nixon* in 1974, and likely several others too. Also, presidential candidates had been hiring lawyers even before campaigns started, long before that year's election.

48. D: Southern opponents of segregation used intimidation and violence against desegregation proponents, and many southern school districts avoided compliance with the new law. The President eventually did have to call in National Guard troops to help with desegregation, but that was a few years later. The Cold War may have started in the 1950s, but did not draw complete attention away from segregation issues.

49. D: Choice A sounds like a good guess, but choice D is the correct answer. Before the *White v. Regester* Supreme Court case, Texas had an "at large" voting system that had weakened minority voting power. The new voting from individual districts would allow more equal representation for heavily Hispanic voting districts, allowing them to have more Hispanic representatives. Choice C would not be correct because the poll tax was outlawed many years before the 1973 case.

50. B: Andrew Carnegie was a wealthy industrialist who, both alone and in cooperation with John Rockefeller, gave money to schools, universities, libraries, and former employees, starting the modern practice of corporate philanthropy in the early 1900s. Henry Ward Beecher was a leader who encouraged wealthy men to donate money to good causes around the same time period. John Stuart Mill was also a contemporary of Carnegie and encouraged donations for education. Elbert H. Gary was Carnegie's partner in a steel company, but not the main impetus behind philanthropic donations. So Andrew Carnegie is the correct answer, and the excerpt is from Carnegie's autobiography.

Practice Test #2

Use the chart and your knowledge of social studies to answer the following question:

ERA in U.S. History	Approximate Dates	Defining Characteristics of this Era
Gilded Age or Progressive Era	1890-1914	The era was called "gilded" because of expanded wealth and prosperity. "Progressive" describes the politics of the time that called for social reforms and eliminating corruption in government.
World War I Era	1914-1918	The U.S. was involved in fighting a war in Europe.
Roaring Twenties	1918-1928	
Great Depression	1929-1940	
World War II Era	1941-1945	
Cold War Era	1945-1964	

1. Which defining characteristic listed below should go in the row for describing the Roaring Twenties Era?

a. After a World War, America wanted to help rebuild Europe and prevent the Soviet Union's possible expansion of communism.
b. After the stock market crash, many businesses failed and unemployment became high.
c. The U.S. was involved in fighting a war with Allies against Germany, Japan, and Italy.
d. The economy was strong with a great demand for new products, while culture in this era, also known as the "Jazz Age," became more experimental.

2. Which Founding Father was governor of Connecticut during and after the Revolutionary War, and was the only governor of a British colony who sided with colonists during the Revolutionary War?

a. Charles Carroll
b. Benjamin Rush
c. Jonathan Trumbull
d. John Witherspoon

Use the map and your knowledge of social studies to answer the following question:

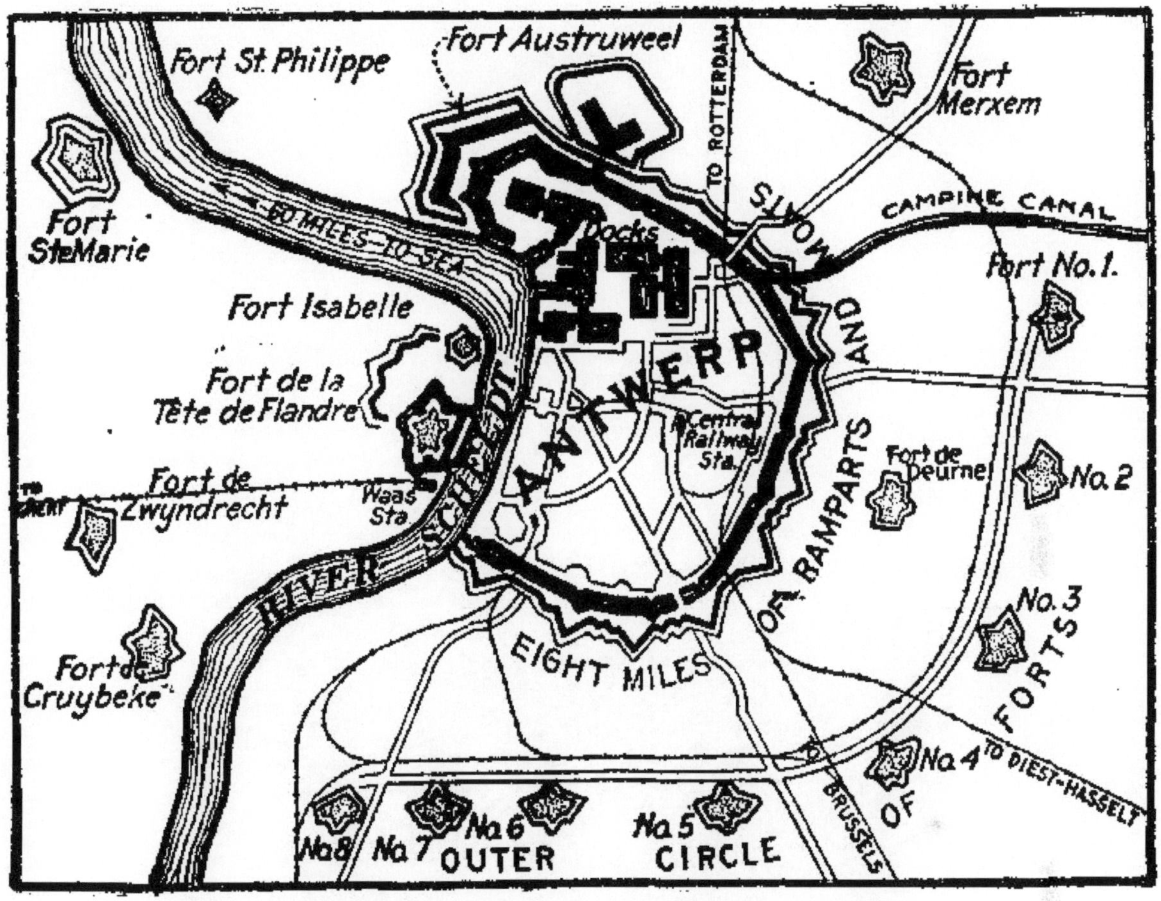

ANTWERP AND ITS FORTIFICATIONS

3. Why was the city of Antwerp in Belgium so heavily fortified in 1914?

a. World War I had started; Germany had invaded other Belgian cities and was going to invade Antwerp also.
b. World War I had started; Italy had invaded other Belgian cities and was going to invade Antwerp also.
c. Antwerp was fortifying against British air attacks that might take place during World War I.
d. Antwerp feared a Russian invasion after the start of World War I.

4. Which choice below lists some contributions to early America made by John Jay?

a. He was the first Chief Justice of New York and also a Minister to France.
b. He signed the Declaration of Independence and was one of the first mayors of New York City.
c. He served in George Washington's army during the Revolution and was Minister to Spain after the war.
d. He was a foreign minister, a contributing writer to the Federalist Papers, and an early governor of New York.

Use the photograph, caption, and your knowledge of social studies to answer the following question:

German Air Raiders over England
In the foreground three British planes are advancing to the attack

5. Based on the photograph and caption from a book about World War I, and your general social studies knowledge, which statement below is MOST likely true?

a. The only airplane warfare during World War I occurred over England.
b. In World War I, American allies had better airplane technology than German allies.
c. Airplane warfare was used in the Civil War before being more widely used in World War I.
d. Airplanes had their first warfare use during World War I, at first just for taking spy photographs, and later for firing guns and dropping bombs.

Use the excerpt and your knowledge of social studies to answer the following question:

> "Perhaps the most characteristic feature of this record of lynch law for the year 1893, is the remarkable fact that five human beings were lynched and that the matter was considered of so little importance that the powerful press bureaus of the country did not consider the matter of enough importance to ascertain the causes for which they were hanged. It tells the world, with perhaps greater emphasis than any other feature of the record, that Lynch Law has become so common in the United States that the finding of the dead body of a Negro, suspended between heaven and earth to the limb of a tree, is of so slight importance that neither the civil authorities nor press agencies consider the matter worth investigating."

6. The above excerpt comes from a book written by a female African-American "muckraker" journalist and reform leader in 1895. What was this author's name?

a. Ella Baker
b. Rosa Parks
c. Sojourner Truth
d. Ida B. Wells

Use the excerpt and your knowledge of social studies to answer the following question:

In *The Great Round World and What Is Going On In It*, a weekly magazine, Sanford B. Dole was interviewed in 1898 about the U.S. plan to annex Hawaii:

> "President Dole made a glowing picture of the benefits that this country would receive from annexation. It would greatly encourage commerce between the United States and Hawaii by making the trade absolutely free, and it would open up to Americans a great many industries, the chief among them being coffee-growing.
>
> "It would also vastly improve the condition of the islands themselves.
>
> In case annexation is rejected by our Government, President Dole says the Hawaiian Government will continue much as it is at present."

7. What was Sanford B. Dole the president of in 1898?

a. The Republic of Hawaii
b. The State of Hawaii
c. The United States
d. The United States Senate

Use the list and your knowledge of social studies to answer the following question:

- It proved that the U.S. was willing to expand its empire and gain resources through imperialism (the taking of colonies).
- It allowed the U.S. to annex Guam, Hawaii, Puerto Rico, and the Philippines.
- It showed the power and strength of the U.S. army and navy.

8. What would be the BEST summarizing title for this list?

a. How the Policies of President Theodore Roosevelt Made the U.S. a World Power
b. How the Spanish-American War Helped the U.S. Become a World Power
c. How the War of 1812 Helped the U.S. Become a World Power
d. How Isolationism Led to Imperialism for the U.S.

Use the excerpt and your knowledge of social studies to answer the following question:

> President Woodrow Wilson's "Fourteen Points" speech in 1918 included the following lines:
>
> "XIV. A general association of nations must be formed under specific covenants for the purpose of affording mutual guarantees of political independence and territorial integrity to great and small states alike.
>
> "In regard to these essential rectifications of wrong and assertions of right we feel ourselves to be intimate partners of all the governments and peoples associated together against the Imperialists. We cannot be separated in interest or divided in

9. Based on this excerpt, what was one way that Wilson's "Fourteen Points" contrasted with his pre-war position of U.S. neutrality?

a. In 1918, Wilson agreed with the philosophy of the imperialists.
b. By 1918, Wilson thought that each nation should form its own government.
c. In this speech, Wilson believed that each nation should be able to decide its own territories.
d. In this speech, Wilson wanted to set up a League of Nations which would eventually become the United Nations.

Use the illustration and your knowledge of social studies to answer the following question:

A sketch from *I Was There...with the Yanks in France* by C. LeRoy Baldridge, written in 1919, shows a sketch of an old trench in the Argonne forest of France

10. Why was the Battle of the Argonne Forest in 1918 difficult and important?

a. The battle was difficult because there was no air support available to the Allies during this time and important because the Allies won anyway.

b. The battle was difficult because there were many Allied prisoners of war hidden in the trenches who needed to be rescued and important because the prisoners were rescued.

c. The battle was difficult because of the deeply forested nature of the area and important because it was the last battle won by the Germans before the end of World War I.

d. The battle was difficult because the Germans were so entrenched in this forest, having built deep trenches there, and important because it was one of the final battles of the war and helped break through Germany's western front.

11. Progressive Era reformers in the early 1900s wanted greater involvement by federal government in public affairs to improve schools, roads, parks, public health, farms, and more. Because government would need money for such reforms, which amendment did Progressives help pass that allowed income tax collection?

a. 16th Amendment
b. 17th Amendment
c. 18th Amendment
d. 19th Amendment

12. In the Progressive Era of the late 1890s and early 1900s, political reformers wanted to make sure government represented the peoples' will. An "initiative" process began in 1898 in South Dakota and then spread to other states. Which definition BEST describes the initiative process?

a. It allowed voting citizens to give their judgment on proposed legislation before state legislators voted on the same legislation.
b. It allowed voters to gather petitions demanding special elections when they wanted to recall an unpopular public official, thereby allowing them to "un-elect" that official.
c. It allowed citizens to introduce legislation proposals at a local or state level by gathering petitions, and proposals would then be addressed by lawmakers or placed on ballots for a vote.
d. It allowed citizens to visit state legislatures and give testimony supporting a certain issue, thereby encouraging the state lawmakers to propose and pass legislation on that same issue.

13. An "Emergency Quota Law" in 1921 was signed by the president to limit new immigrants to the U.S. was most likely an effect of which popular philosophy of the time period?

a. Harlem Renaissance, which showed that African Americans had much to contribute to society and should be given jobs before letting in more immigrants.
b. Nativism, a belief that native-born Americans, especially white Americans, were superior to foreign-born Americans.
c. Prohibition, a belief that alcohol was un-American because beer was mostly brewed by German-Americans, and thus immigration of Germans and other Europeans with alcohol as part of their cultural traditions should be limited.
d. Women's Suffrage Movement, arguing that women should get rights before more immigrants were let in the U.S.

Use the timeline and your knowledge of social studies to answer the following question:

> *Dec. 7, 1941* - Pearl Harbor in Hawaii is bombed by Japan. The FBI arrests some Japanese-American community leaders who are held away from their families.
>
> *Dec. 8, 1941* - U.S. Congress declares war on Japan.
>
> *Feb. 19, 1942* - President Franklin D. Roosevelt signs Executive Order 9066, ordering military areas off-limits to certain people.
>
> *March 18, 1942* - President Roosevelt signs Executive Order 9102, which establishes a "War Relocation Authority."

14. What event would BEST go next in this timeline's factual sequence of events?

a. Thousands of Japanese-American men, women and children are relocated from the U.S. west coast for east coast locations.
b. All Japanese-American men are denied the chance to be U.S. soldiers for the duration of World War II.
c. Thousands of Japanese-American men, women and children are relocated to internment camps.
d. Many Japanese-American men have their passports confiscated and are forced to leave the U.S.

15. In May 1991, the First International Gathering of Children Hidden during World War II held a meeting in New York City. Around 1,600 former hidden children attended this meeting. Which of the following is the BEST explanation for why these adults had to be hidden as children in Europe during World War II?

a. They were in danger of being drafted into youth army groups in fascist Germany.
b. They were hiding from war zones and waiting for fake passports to take them to Israel.
c. They had to be hidden from French families who would have taken them away from their original homelands to adopt them.
d. They were Jewish and had to be hidden from Nazis in order to survive the Holocaust, the attempted extermination of the Jewish population by Nazi Germany.

Use the photo and your knowledge of social studies to answer the following question:

Damage Inspection: *A squadron operations officer of the 332d Fighter Group points out a cannon hole to ground crew, Italy, 1945*

16. Besides being called the "332nd Fighter Group," what was another name for those fighter pilots in World War II?

a. Flying Tigers
b. Red Barons
c. Top Guns
d. Tuskegee Airmen

17. Why did the North Atlantic Treaty Organization (NATO) form with a military alliance between the U.S. and several European countries in 1949?

a. It formed to defend against communist Soviet Union which had taken over some central and eastern European countries.
b. It formed to combine with the work of the United Nations in policing war-ravaged areas of the third world.
c. NATO formed to combat international terrorism and regulate nuclear weapons.
d. NATO formed to defend against a re-united Germany.

18. The "Domino Theory," first suggested by President Dwight Eisenhower but also followed by presidents after him, claimed that if one nation in Asia became a communist country, then other Asian countries would follow soon afterwards, like a set of dominoes. The U.S. fought a war in which country because of this theory?

a. Burma
b. China
c. Thailand
d. Vietnam

19. By autumn of 1967, 93 percent of American homes had a television. Most of the evening news was reporting about the Vietnam War, and about 50 million Americans watched the news each night. What was an effect of these media developments?

a. The views of war action inspired many men to register for the draft.
b. Positive media coverage of the war's progress resulted in an increase of American support for the war.
c. News with graphic images and interviews with frustrated soldiers resulted in a decrease of American public support for the war.
d. Although Walter Cronkite, a trusted television news anchor, supported the U.S. staying in the war, Americans started to decide it was not a good idea to stay in Vietnam.

20. Which social activist helped start a union for workers' rights in 1962 called the *National Farm Workers Association* (NFWA)?

a. Cesar Chavez
b. Felix Longoria
c. Hector P. Garcia
d. Martin Luther King, Jr.

Use the excerpt and your knowledge of social studies to answer the following question:

Excerpt from *The Black Experience in America* by Norman Coombs, 1972:

"In November [of 1963], Congressional debate on the Civil Rights Bill was still continuing, but the President had now made the passage of the Civil Rights Bill one of the most urgent goals of his Administration. But on the 22nd of November, John F. Kennedy was gunned down in the Presidential limousine in Dallas, Texas. The nation and the world were struck dumb with disbelief. Even those who had disliked his politics were horrified at the assassination of a President in a democratic state. His supporters felt that they had lost a friend as well as a leader...

The sense of shock caused despair and gloom. The fact that his successor, Lyndon B. Johnson, was a Southerner led most civil rights supporters to feel that there would be a reversal of federal policies on the racial question. However, Johnson immediately tried to reassure the nation that his intention was to carry on with the unfinished business of the Kennedy era."

21. Based on this excerpt and your knowledge of social studies, what could be predicted would happen next in history?

a. President Johnson did sign a Civil Rights Act, but not until 1967.
b. Congress passed a Civil Rights Act in 1964, and President Johnson signed it.
c. Congress passed a Civil Rights Act in 1964, but President Johnson did not sign it.
d. Without the leadership of President Kennedy, congress did not pass a Civil Rights Act until the 1970s.

Use the chart and your knowledge of social studies to answer the following question:

Participants	Date	Agreements Made
Israeli Prime Minister Menachem Begin (signer)	1979	Israel agreed to return the Sinai to Egypt
Egyptian President Anwar el-Sadat (signer)		Egypt and Israel agreed to work on Palestinian independence steps for the West Bank and Gaza
US President Jimmy Carter (Witness)		

22. What would be the BEST title for this chart?

a. Arab Spring Agreements
b. Camp David Accords
c. Palestine Liberation Organization Treaty
d. Peace through Strength Plans

Use the excerpt and your knowledge of social studies to answer the following question:

Excerpt from *The Black Experience in America* by Norman Coombs, 1972

"He held that, when the rights of blacks were violated, they should be willing to die in the struggle to secure them:

"If white America doesn't think the Afro-American, especially the upcoming generation, is capable of adopting the guerrilla tactics now being used by oppressed people elsewhere on this earth, she is making a drastic mistake. She is underestimating the force that can do her the most harm.

"A real honest effort to remove the just grievances of the 22 million Afro-Americans must be made immediately or in a short time it will be too late."

"The slogan 'Black Power' exploded from a public address system in Greenwood, Mississippi, in the summer of 1966…"

23. Which historical figure was MOST likely the speaker of the long quote in this excerpt (the one that starts "If white America…")?

a. James Meredith
b. Malcolm X
c. Martin Luther King, Jr.
d. William Clay

Use the list and your knowledge of social studies to answer the following question:

Jobs
Land
Political freedoms
Religious freedoms

24. What is the BEST explanation for what the items on this list all had in common during the late 1800s?

a. These were all promises of President Theodore Roosevelt's administration
b. These were all reasons why immigrants came to America in hopes of better lives
c. These were all reasons why settlers made a rush to California and other western states
d. These were all things offered by the government to Native Americans at that time period

Use the excerpt and your knowledge of social studies to answer the following question:

> "The earnestness of the Americans in the situation was proclaimed to the world by the English and French, and General Pershing placed his name and that of his country and men high on the wall of fame by unselfishly offering to France at the most critical period the use of his entire force, to be disposed of and assigned wherever General Foch and his staff decided to use them. Within a few days thereafter the American troops which had been in training were marched in to relieve the stressed English and French."

25. The author of this excerpt is describing a turning point in which war?

a. War of 1812
b. Spanish-American War
c. World War I
d. World War II

26. Who headed the National Association for the Advancement of Colored People (NAACP) in 1910, founded and edited the NAACP's journal *The Crisis*, and wrote many "muckraking" articles for *The Crisis* about civil rights for African Americans?

a. W.E.B. DuBois
b. Matthew Gaines
c. Marcus Garvey
d. Booker T. Washington

27. Which reason or reasons BEST explain why the U.S. Office of War Information included famous stars such as Ethel Merman in their radio broadcasts in the 1940s?

a. To build morale, raise spirits, and help convince women they needed to stay home while men went to war
b. To build morale, raise spirits, and help convince women to apply for wartime work
c. To convince women to buy tickets to Broadway shows to support the U.S. economy during wartime
d. To convince women to buy movie tickets to support the U.S. economy during wartime

Use the excerpt and your knowledge of social studies to answer the following question:

> "As you know, I will soon be visiting the People's Republic of China and the Soviet Union. I go there with no illusions. We have great differences with both powers. We shall continue to have great differences. But peace depends on the ability of great powers to live together on the same planet despite their differences."

28. Which president gave this speech, as he was about to become the first U.S. President to visit the communist People's Republic of China?

a. President John F. Kennedy
b. President Lyndon B. Johnson
c. President Richard M. Nixon
d. President Gerald R. Ford

29. What event in April 1975 meant that the Vietnam War was over and that South Vietnam would surrender to the communists, leading to the eventual reunification of the country under communist rule?

a. Fall of Saigon
b. Ho Chi Minh's death
c. My Lai Massacre
d. Tet Offensive

30. "Old enough to fight, old enough to vote" became a slogan for a youth voting rights movement after the World War II military draft age was lowered to 18, while 21 remained the minimum voting age. The Vietnam War draft brought more urgency to the youth voting rights movement and resulted in which amendment to lower the voting age to 18?

a. 24th Amendment
b. 25th Amendment
c. 26th Amendment
d. 27th Amendment

Use the list and your knowledge of social studies to answer the following question:

Poor agricultural practices
Years of drought
Lack of ground cover to hold soil in place
High winds on the plains

31. What would be the BEST title to summarize this list?

a. Causes of the 1935 Dust Bowl
b. Effects of the 1935 Dust Bowl
c. Issues for the 1970s Era Rust Belt
d. Issues for the 1970s Era Sun Belt

Use the excerpt and your knowledge of social studies to answer the following question:

Excerpt from *Crossing the Plains, Days of '57* by William Audley Maxwell, 1915

"We forded the Platte at a point something like one hundred and fifty miles westward from its confluence with the Missouri. There was no road leading into the river, nor any evidence of its having been crossed by any one at that place. We were informed that the bottom was of quicksand, and fording, therefore, dangerous. We tested it, by riding horses across. Contrary to our expectations, the bottom was found to be a surface of smooth sand, packed hard enough to bear up the wagons, when the movement was quick and continuous. A cut was made in the bank, to form a runway for passage of the wagons to the water's edge; and the whole train crossed the stream safely, with no further mishap than the wetting of a driver and the dipping of a wagon into a place deep enough to let water into the box. Fording the Platte consumed one entire day. We camped that night on the north shore."

32. Which statement BEST summarizes the main idea of the above paragraph describing geographic factors for settlers headed to the Great Plains?

a. Fording the Platte River in stage coach wagons was dangerous because wagons often got caught in quicksand
b. Fording the Platte River was believed to be dangerous, but it turned out to be quick and easy for stage coach wagons
c. Fording the Platte River was thought to be dangerous, but it turned out to be mostly time-consuming and a little inconvenient
d. After fording the Platte River, stage coach wagons could continue driving west or could stop and camp for a night by the shore of the river

Use the chart and your knowledge of social studies to answer the following question:

US Census Data

(All population figures are per 200,000 square miles of land area)

Date	Northeastern US Rural Areas	Northeastern US Urban Areas
1890	Population average of around 7.5 million	Population average of around 12.5 million
1930	Population average of around 11 million	Population average of around 30 million

33. Which conclusion is MOST likely true based on this U.S. Census Data chart?

a. Rural to urban migration was a probable trend between the years 1890 and 1930.
b. Urban to rural migration was a probable pattern between the years 1890 and 1930.
c. Urban areas grew in population numbers but rural areas had a decreased population between 1890 and 1930.
d. Rural areas grew in population numbers but urban areas had a decreased population between 1890 and 1930.

Use the timeline and your knowledge of social studies to answer the following question:

1962 - The book "Silent Spring," by Rachel Carson, was published and soon became a bestseller. The book exposed the negative effects of pesticides on the environment in the U.S.

1969 - President Nixon set up a Cabinet-level "Environmental Quality Council" as well as a "Citizens' Advisory Committee on Environmental Quality."

1970 - In February, President Nixon announced stronger federal programs to deal with water and air pollution.

1970 - In April that year, the first Earth Day was celebrated in the U.S. by about 20 million Americans.

34. Based on this timeline, which event MOST likely took place in December of 1970?

a. Future Vice President Al Gore gave a report on global warming to his fellow college students
b. Vietnam War protests overshadowed the public concern for a healthy environment and the issue faded away for a while
c. President Nixon oversaw the establishment of the National Park System, setting aside lands for protection and public recreation
d. President Nixon oversaw the establishment of the Environmental Protection Agency to consolidate pollution control and environmental protection

35. "Sustainable development" is defined as development that meets the needs of the present while still making possible the ability of future generations to meet their needs. It takes into account environmental impacts and tries to minimize damage to the environment. Which reason BEST describes why there is a need for sustainable development?

a. The environment will always evolve to adapt to the needs of future generations
b. Future generations will not have as many scientists because education is deteriorating
c. Population growth has stabilized, but there are still future stresses on the environment such as global warming
d. The continued forecasted population growth can damage the environment with greater stresses on oceans, food supplies, and land

36. In the 1960s, "Beat Generation" member Allen Ginsberg worked with psychologist Timothy Leary to promote more widespread use of the drug LSD. What was an impact of this on American society?

a. More widespread use made the drug LSD more popular and it became a legal drug.
b. LSD was a legal drug until the 1980s "War on Drugs" made it an illegal substance.
c. Politicians were some people who experimented with LSD and it made them more open-minded about political issues.
d. While some people may have felt that LSD was psychologically helpful, many people experienced bad effects such as fear or psychosis from the drug, and the drug was and is still illegal.

Use the excerpt and your knowledge of social studies to answer the following question:

> In this excerpt from *The Black Experience in America* (1972), author Norman Coombs describes the 1920s Harlem Renaissance:
>
> "Students, peasants, artists, businessmen, professional men, poets, musicians, and workers; all came to Harlem...Langston Hughes, in describing his first entrance into Harlem from the 135th Street subway exit, said that he felt vitality and hope throbbing in the air. In Black Manhattan, James Weldon Johnson said that Harlem was not a slum or a fringe. Rather, he insisted that it was one of the "most beautiful and healthful sections of the city."

37. Based on the excerpt, what was one probable impact of the Harlem Renaissance for African-American society?

a. It made African Americans feel like they were relegated to a ghetto culture
b. It gave African Americans a new sense of pride and confidence in their culture
c. The Harlem Renaissance made black people feel like they should only live in the Harlem area of Manhattan and not in any other cities
d. The Harlem Renaissance was helpful for black artists, musicians, and writers, but not for businessmen or other professional black people

Use the list and your knowledge of social studies to answer the following question:

- Islamic rap groups in England and France
- A Basque group in Spain called Negu Gorriak that incorporates U.S. hip-hop
- Musicians in New Zealand who combine rap, soul and reggae with traditional Maori music

38. What is the BEST generalization that could be made based on this list?

a. American culture can spread globally through entertainment such as rap and hip-hop music, but that same culture sometimes gets reconstituted into new forms in other countries
b. Rap and hip-hop music have spread from the U.S. to Spain, England, France, and New Zealand, but not to any other countries
c. Rap and hip-hop music are examples of ways that Hollywood influences culture in other countries
d. Rap and hip-hop music arose originally in other countries before becoming popular in the U.S.

39. Which choice BEST shows the contributions of Italian-American women to U.S. culture in the field of politics?

a. Sylvia Scaramelli helped co-found a college in New Jersey in 1942; Suzette Charles (born Suzette De Gaetano) was the first Italian American to win the Miss America title
b. The first woman to run for Vice President of the United States was Geraldine Ferraro in 1984; the first woman elected governor in her own right was Ella T. Grasso of Connecticut in 1975
c. Jerre Mangione wrote about the history of Italian Americans; Dr. Rosemarie Truglio studied the effects of television on children and teenagers
d. Sonia Sotomayor is a current female Supreme Court Justice; Don DeLillo is an Italian-American author

40. In which movement were members of the Quaker religious group NOT very active?

a. Abolitionist movement
b. McCarthyism movement
c. Pacifist and peace activist movements
d. Women's rights movement

41. Which First Lady was honorary vice chair of the Red Cross and led blood donation and fundraising drives during a war?

a. Edith Bolling Galt Wilson
b. Eleanor Roosevelt
c. Lady Bird Johnson
d. Pat Nixon

42. More than one elementary school in Texas is named after Roy Benavidez, a Mexican American born in Texas, and he was buried with full military honors at Fort Sam Houston National Cemetery. Why?

a. He was the first Mexican American to serve in the army and become a state senator in Texas
b. He was the first Mexican American to become a high-ranking officer in the army in the 1950s
c. He won a Congressional Medal of Honor for his brave military service during the Korean War
d. He won a Congressional Medal of Honor and a Purple Heart for his brave military service and actions in the Vietnam War

43. When the FBI examined homes of Japanese Americans without warrants during World War II, which constitutional right of those Japanese Americans was violated?

a. Right to reasonable bail
b. Freedom of the press
c. Freedom from unreasonable searches and seizures
d. Right to a speedy and public trial

44. How did all Native Americans achieve U.S. citizenship?

a. By marrying white American citizens
b. By serving in American military units
c. By studying for and passing a citizenship test
d. Through passage of the American Indian Citizenship Act of 1924

Use the excerpt and your knowledge of social studies to answer the following question:

Excerpt from *Integration of the Armed Forces, 1940-1965*, by Morris J. MacGregor, Jr.

"The laws of 1866 and 1869 that guaranteed the existence of four black Regular Army regiments also institutionalized segregation, granting federal recognition to a system racially separate and theoretically equal in treatment and opportunity a generation before the Supreme Court sanctioned such a distinction in *Plessy* v. *Ferguson*."

45. Which option BEST describes what was sanctioned by the Supreme Court in the *Plessy v. Ferguson* case of 1896?

a. Segregation, or the idea of separate but equal treatment for African Americans
b. Integration and equal treatment for African Americans
c. Army regiments that had a majority of black servicemen
d. Army regiments that had only black servicemen

46. In the 1954 *Hernandez v. Texas* case, the Supreme Court decided that white and Hispanic could be considered different "classes" because of the way Hispanics had been unfairly treated in Texas. What was a MAIN effect of this decision?

a. Hispanics accused of crimes still faced juries composed only of white Americans
b. African Americans also started to be considered as a different class, instead of as a different race
c. Hispanics were now an identifiable minority group and their segregation could be prohibited under the *Brown* decision of 1954
d. Civil rights activists used the different class concept as their legal strategy for the next several decades, and the 14th Amendment was now applied to Hispanics as well as to African Americans

47. If a high school student wanted to wear an armband to protest the U.S. military presence in Afghanistan, which Supreme Court decision could the student cite as allowing him or her to wear that armband into school (as long as the student did not disrupt classes)?

a. *Hazelwood School District v. Kuhlmeier*, 1988
b. *Bethel School District No. 403 v. Fraser*, 1986
c. *Tinker v. Des Moines*, 1969
d. *Doremus v. Board of Education of Borough of Hawthorne*, 1952

48. In 1937, President Franklin D. Roosevelt was accused by opponents of trying to "pack the court," and his plan for courts was defeated by the U.S. Senate. What was Roosevelt's plan for the judicial branch at that time?

a. Roosevelt wanted only Democrats to be appointed to federal district courts
b. Roosevelt wanted only Democrats to be appointed as Supreme Court justices
c. Roosevelt wanted to raise the total number of Supreme Court justices from nine to 15
d. Roosevelt wanted to raise the total number of federal district court judges from 94 to 100

49. Which choice below BEST shows an example of how one can "lobby" a congressperson?

a. Voting for your congressperson during an election campaign
b. Voting for your congressperson's opponent during an election
c. Reading the email newsletters your congressperson sends to supporters
d. Writing a letter to your congressperson about an issue that is important to you

Question 50 pertains to the following excerpt from *The Black Experience in America*, author Norman Coombs describes a 1960s sit-in:

> "In a matter of weeks, student sit-ins were occurring at segregated lunch counters all across the South. College and high school students by the thousands joined the Civil Rights Movement. These students felt the need to form their own organization to mobilize and facilitate the spontaneous demonstrations which were springing up everywhere."

50. Student "sit-ins" are BEST described as which kind of way to participate in the democratic process?

a. Displaying Black Power to incite fear
b. Litigating
c. Lobbying
d. Non-violent protesting

Answer Key and Explanations for Test #2

1. D: It gives the correct defining characteristic of the Roaring Twenties Era. The economy was strong with a great demand for new products, while culture in this era, also known as the "Jazz Age," became more experimental. A student might pick choice A, which defines the Cold War Era, if he or she focuses on the fact that it is also an era immediately following a World War. A student can rule out the other choices if they know how to correctly define the World War II and Great Depression Eras.

2. C: Jonathan Trumbull is the correct answer for which Founding Father was governor of Connecticut during and after the Revolutionary War. The other names are all of Founding Fathers, but none were governor of Connecticut. Rush, Witherspoon and Carroll all signed the Declaration of Independence; Carroll was a U.S. Senator for Maryland while Rush lived in Pennsylvania and Witherspoon in New Jersey.

3. A: It shows the student's knowledge of the importance of 1914 events as a turning point for the start of World War I in Europe: "World War I had started; Germany had invaded other Belgian cities and was going to invade Antwerp also." The other choices are incorrect because Italy, Russia, and England were not invading Belgium.

4. D: It lists true contributions by John Jay to early. Choice A is partly correct about the first Chief Justice, but Jay was a Minister to Spain, not to France. Choice B correctly places him in New York, but he did not sign the Declaration or become mayor of New York City. Choice C has Minister of Spain correct, but Jay did not serve in George Washington's army during the war.

5. D: While the photo shows World War I airplane warfare over England, it also took place over other countries like Germany and France, so choice A is incorrect. Airplane warfare first took place after the invention of the airplane, so during the Civil War could not be a correct choice. The American allies and the German side went back and forth in terms of airplane technology superiority, so choice B is not correct. Choice D is the MOST likely answer choice. Airplanes had their first warfare use during WWI, at first just for taking spy photographs, but were also used later in the war for firing guns and dropping bombs. The photo illustrates the fact that airplanes were in use during WWI for firing guns and dropping bombs.

6. D: Ella Baker was a civil rights leader but born in 1903. Rosa Parks was part of the 1960s civil rights movement. Sojourner Truth lived near the time of Ida B. Wells, but she had died by 1883. Ida B. Wells is the correct answer, and she was known as a journalist, muckraker, reform leader, and fighter against lynchings.

7. A: Sanford B. Dole was the President of the Republic of Hawaii, and he did argue for annexation of Hawaii by the United States. Students familiar with the time period should know that he was not the President of the United States or the President of the U.S. Senate. The excerpt may help them realize this fact. Also, Hawaii did not become a state officially until the 1950s, so choice B is incorrect.

8. B: The BEST summarizing title for the list is "How the Spanish-American War Helped the U.S. Become a World Power." President Theodore Roosevelt did help the U.S. become a world power, but that was after the events on the list (Spanish-American War events) because he was not president until 1901, after the war of 1898. Isolationism did give way to Imperialism in the 1890s, but it did not lead to or cause imperialism. The War of 1812 is an incorrect answer for students who know their historical dates and war events.

9. D: In point 14 of his 1918 speech Wilson was proposing a League of Nations which would eventually become the United Nations. If the student reads the excerpt carefully, and knows general history about the United Nations, the student will know that having the U.S. involved in such a league would be a contrast to Wilson's pre-War policy of neutrality. The other choices given make references to phrases found in the excerpt, but they are not statements that contrast with a policy of neutrality and are incorrect answer choices.

10. D: It is correct for why the Battle of the Argonne Forest was difficult and important. The illustration gives a clue to the answer because it shows a deep trench (though it also shows a forest, so the student also needs general social studies knowledge). The battle was difficult because the Germans were so entrenched in this forest, having built deep trenches there; and important because it was one of the final battles of the war and helped break through Germany's western front. The deeply forested nature of the area mentioned in choice C was also a difficulty, but that choice is incorrect because it claims the Germans won that battle when they did not. Some German soldiers were taken as prisoners of war during the battle, and there may have been some Allied prisoners, but that was not the purpose of the battle. There was air support provided to the Allies in that battle, so choice A is incorrect.

11. A: The 16th Amendment is the correct answer for which amendment dealt with collecting income taxes to help fund progressive government goals. While all the amendments listed were championed by Progressive Era reformers, and all were around the same time period, the other amendments listed dealt with voting issues or prohibition, not with income taxes.

12. C: It is the BEST and only definition of the initiative process: It allowed citizens to introduce legislation proposals at a local or state level by gathering petitions, and proposals would then be addressed by lawmakers or placed on ballots for a vote. The other answer choices give definitions of "referendum" (choice A), "recall" (choice B), and also describe simply visiting a state legislature to give testimony about an issue (choice D), none of which define the "initiative" process.

13. B: "Nativism," a philosophy of the time period that native-born white Americans were superior to foreign born Americans, helped cause the Emergency Quota Act that limited immigrants in 1921. The other options were all social issues of the same time period, but not the main cause for limiting immigration. The Harlem Renaissance and Women's Suffrage Movement did not have such qualms with immigrants. Prohibition was partly caused by anti-immigrant sentiment such as against Germans after WWI, but Prohibition did not cause the Quota Act as much as Nativism.

14. C: It would BEST go next in the timeline's factual sequence of events because the other choices are not factually correct: thousands of Japanese-American men, women and children are relocated to internment camps. They were not forced to leave the U.S., and they were not forced to move from west coast to east coast (many internment camps were on the west coast). Japanese-American men did eventually start to be drafted for military service during World War II, and many did fight in that war for the U.S.

15. D: It is the correct answer for this particular group of children, although choices A and B might be good guesses. There were German youth who wanted to avoid serving in Nazi armies, but they did not go into hiding in as great numbers as did Jewish youth trying to escape the Holocaust. There were children who awaited fake passports, but mostly to escape to the U.S. or other safe countries, as Israel was not founded until after World War II. The correct answer is that "They were Jewish and had to be hidden from Nazis in order to survive the Holocaust, the attempted extermination of the Jewish population by Nazi Germany."

16. D: The Tuskegee Airmen was another name for the 332nd Fighter Group. The African-American men in the photo give the clue that it was the Tuskegee Airmen and not the Flying Tigers, who were Chinese American. The Tuskegee Airmen were an African-American group of fighter pilots in WWII, which should be general social studies knowledge at this grade level. Red Barons were in WWI, and Top Guns are navy pilots, nicknamed in a later time period than WWII.

17. A: NATO formed for the purpose of defending Europe from possible encroachment by communist Soviet Union armies which had invaded and were controlling some central and eastern European countries after WWII. Choice B and C may have eventually become other purposes for NATO in later years, but were not the original reasons for the formation of NATO. Choice D is incorrect because Germany did not immediately reunite after the war.

18. D: The Vietnam War was fought by the U.S. in Vietnam because of the Domino Theory. China was the "first domino" in the theory, in that it became a communist nation before other Asian countries, but the U.S. did not fight a war there. The U.S. has also had shaky relations with Burma more recently, but did not fight a war there or in Thailand.

19. C: It is the correct result from the increased media coverage and availability. News with graphic images and interviews with frustrated soldiers resulted in a decrease of American public support for the war. It did not result in increased American support or in more men registering for the draft. The choice about Walter Cronkite could be a good guess, except that in 1970 Cronkite declared the war a "bloody stalemate," thus echoing and influencing the opinions of a majority of Americans about the Vietnam War.

20. A: Cesar Chavez, along with Dolores Huerta and Gilbert Padilla, helped start the NFWA in 1962. Students who know a little about Chavez and his lifelong activism for Hispanic migrant workers should be able to choose the correct answer. A student might incorrectly pick Hector P. Garcia or Felix Longoria for being others from the Mexican American civil rights movements (Garcia a doctor, and Longoria a WWII soldier). Or a student might pick Martin Luther King, Jr. because he also helped workers form unions, although not as much for farmers as for urban city workers.

21. B: The excerpt states that Johnson did want to carry on Kennedy's agenda and legacy, and that included in the field of Civil Rights, despite Johnson originally being a southerner. So the correct answer is B, Congress passed a Civil Rights Act in 1964 and President Johnson signed it. Students reading the excerpt carefully and having a good general knowledge of civil rights history should be able to make that correct prediction.

22. B: The Camp David Accords is the correct name for this historical event which included the 1979 leaders of Egypt and Israel making agreements with both the help and witnessing of U.S. President Jimmy Carter. The Arab Spring is a more current event (2010-2011), and Peace through Strength was a Reagan-era philosophy. Palestinians are mentioned in the Camp David Accords, so choice C could be a good guess, but general social studies knowledge of the Middle East should help students remember that the PLO is Yasser Arafat's organization.

23. B: Malcolm X is the correct speaker of the excerpt's long quotation, as he is the only one on the list from the Black Power movement. James Sherman did a Freedom March and was murdered, which inspired some Black Power rallies, but he himself was not the advocate of a less peaceful movement. Martin Luther King, Jr. was the main advocate of nonviolent social change, so he would not have spoken the quote about "guerrilla tactics." William Clay was a representative and leader of the Black Caucus in Congress, not a revolutionary figure.

24. B: Jobs, land, and religious and political freedoms were all reasons why immigrants imagined that they would have better lives by coming to America in the late 1800s. Theodore Roosevelt was not president until 1901. Native Americans were not promised all of these things during that time period, or at least that would not be the BEST answer. Settlers did rush to California and the west for land, but not for the other items on that list, and gold is not on the list, which makes that choice a poor answer option.

25. C: The clue in the excerpt about American troops helping the stressed French and British troops should let the student know that the excerpt refers to World War I or World War II. If they read closely enough to see General Pershing's involvement, then they should know from general social studies knowledge at this grade level that Pershing was the commander of American Expeditionary Forces during World War I, and therefore C is the correct answer.

26. A: W.E.B. DuBois was a famous African American muckraking journalist for the NAACP's magazine in the early 1900s. Booker T. Washington was a contemporary of DuBois, but not a muckraking journalist. Gaines was a former slave who became a Texas State Senator, but Gaines died in 1900 and therefore could not be the correct answer. Marcus Garvey had a writing career advocating civil rights, but in a newspaper he started called *The Negro World*.

27. B: Students who know about the U.S. Office of War Information should know that the purpose was to get out messages that would build morale and raise spirits. They also tried to recruit women for wartime work during WWII. They sometimes used famous stars such as Ethel Merman to further appeal to women. Their purpose was not to sell Broadway or movie tickets, nor was it to encourage women to stay at home.

28. C: The speech is from President Richard M. Nixon, who was about to become, in 1972, the first U.S. president to visit the People's Republic of China. The other presidents listed are good guesses as they are from similar time periods and might have made similar speeches about China and the Soviet Union, but they are incorrect choices.

29. A: The Fall of Saigon happened in April 1975 and marked the end of the Vietnam War and the beginning of Vietnam's reunification under communist rule. A student might pick one of the other events because they were all events that did happen in the course of the Vietnam War, but they happened on earlier dates, not in April 1975, and were not the final event that marked the end of the war or South Vietnam's surrender.

30. C: The 26th Amendment is the youth voting rights amendment allowing 18-year-olds to vote, signed by President Nixon. The Vietnam War gave more urgency to the "old enough to fight, old enough to vote" slogan. The other amendment choices are in similar time frames and close enough to the 26th Amendment to possibly confuse a student who has not fully studied some of the more important amendments such as the 26th.

31. A: It is the BEST title for the list, The Causes of the 1935 Dust Bowl. The lack of ground cover was a cause of the Dust Bowl, but could also be considered a possible effect of dust storms also. But that is the only item on the list that would also be an effect of the Dust Bowl. The Sun Belt also had some years of drought, but the other items would not fit for Sun Belt as much, or for the Rust Belt except for possibly poor agricultural practices.

32. C: It is the BEST summary of the paragraph's main idea for settlers headed to the Great Plains in stage coach wagons: Fording the Platte River was thought to be dangerous, but turned out to mostly be time-consuming and a little inconvenient: time consuming because it "consumed" a whole day and inconvenient in that drivers and wagon boxes got wet. Choice A is incorrect because the wagon in the paragraph did not get caught in quicksand. Choice B is incorrect because it was not a quick and easy fording (it consumed a whole day). Choice D is a correct and true statement, but it has to do with a detail of the trip after the river crossing, and does not deal with the paragraph's main idea of describing the river crossing.

33. A: The most likely conclusion based on the U.S. Census data chart is that rural to urban migration was a probable trend between the years 1890 and 1930. Both rural and urban areas grew in population numbers, making choices C and D incorrect, but urban areas grew by a much larger margin, meaning that there was probably migration from rural areas in addition to general population growth as a factor for the different numbers. Choice B is incorrect because urban to rural migration numbers are not shown on the chart.

34. D: Choice A is incorrect because Al Gore was not yet speaking on global warming issues during that time period. Choice B does not make sense in the context of the timeline because all the other events listed deal with environmental issues. Choice C confuses the establishment of the National Park System with the EPA. The park system was established earlier by Theodore Roosevelt, which should be part of the student's general social studies knowledge. Choice D is correct: Nixon established the EPA in December 1970.

35. D: It is the best reason why sustainable development is needed: The continued, forecasted population growth can damage the environment with greater stresses on oceans, food supplies, and land. Even though global warming (mentioned in choice C) is another reason why sustainable development is needed, the statement in choice C that population growth has stabilized is false. Fertility rates have fallen in some areas, but the world population will continue to expand for many years before possibly stabilizing. Choices A and B are not completely true statements and not good reasons for sustainable development.

36. D: A student picking answer D shows an understanding of a negative impact of the Beat Generation promoting the drug LSD: While some people may have felt that LSD was psychologically helpful, many people experienced bad effects such as fear or psychosis from the drug, and the drug was and still is illegal. The drug has been illegal since 1966, so choices A and B are incorrect. Choice C is also incorrect in that politicians were not the main people influenced by the Beat Generation to experiment with the drug.

37. B: Reading the excerpt and the proud quotes in it about Harlem should lead students to the correct answer about the impact of the Harlem Renaissance on African-American society in the 1920s: it gave African Americans a new sense of pride and confidence in their culture. It did not make them feel relegated to a "ghetto," as they chose to live in Harlem and made it a nice place to live. But blacks also lived in other cities, making choice C incorrect. Choice D is incorrect because the first part of the excerpt describes all kinds of people coming to participate in the Harlem Renaissance, not just artists, musicians, and writers, as might be popularly thought to be true.

38. A: It is the right choice for a generalization based on the bulleted list: American culture can spread globally through entertainment such as rap and hip-hop music, but that same culture sometimes gets reconstituted into new forms in other countries. Choice B is incorrect because rap and hip-hop have spread from the U.S. to other countries also. Hollywood was not the main medium for spreading rap and hip-hop, since they are forms of music and not films, making choice C incorrect. Choice D is incorrect because rap and hip-hop mostly originated in the U.S.

39. B: It best shows contributions of Italian-American women in the field of politics: The first woman to run for U.S. Vice President was Geraldine Ferraro in 1984, and the first woman elected governor in her own right was Ella T. Grasso of Connecticut in 1975. The other choices show Italian-American women (or in one case a Latina woman, Sonia Sotomayor) making contributions in other fields that are not as political (education, Miss America, etc.). Some of the names listed are actually Italian-American men: Don DeLillo and Jerre Mangione.

40. B: Students with general social studies knowledge at this grade level will have heard of the Quaker religious group, who were active in the Abolitionist movement, women's rights movement, and pacifist/peace movements throughout U.S. history, because all those movements agree with their religious views on equality and peace. The correct answer of B, the McCarthyism movement, is therefore an example of one movement that Quakers were NOT as involved in. In fact, Edward R. Murrow, one of the biggest opponents of McCarthy's "Un-American Activities Committee," was raised as a Quaker.

41. B: Eleanor Roosevelt was the First Lady who was also an honorary chair of the Red Cross. However, all of the First Ladies listed were First Ladies during war times, so they could be good guesses. But a student who knows the particular contributions of Eleanor Roosevelt to American politics and society should know the correct answer.

42. D: It best explains the fame and military burial honors for Mexican-American Roy Benavidez: He won a Congressional Medal of Honor and a Purple Heart for his brave military service and actions in the Vietnam War. He did serve in the Korean War briefly, but did not win his awards for that service. Choices A and B are false statements.

43. C: The freedom from unreasonable search and seizure was the constitutional right violated by the FBI when they searched the homes of Japanese Americans without search warrants during World War II. The other rights may have been violated in other ways by the government at the same time (also against Japanese Americans), but not in this particular given example. A student that understands the Constitution will answer correctly.

44. D: All Native Americans were granted U.S. citizenship by the American Indian Citizenship Act of 1924. Having to take a citizenship test sounds correct, as many immigrants do that today, but it is not the correct answer. It is correct that some Native Americans achieved citizenship by marrying white citizens or by serving in the U.S. military, but not all Native Americans became citizens until passage of the act in 1924.

45. A: A student reading the excerpt closely and knowing their general social studies history about *Plessy v. Ferguson* will choose the correct answer for what it decreed: segregation, or the idea of separate but equal treatment, for African Americans. A student might be fooled by the book title's "integration" mention to choose answer B. Or they may focus on the mention of black servicemen in the excerpt and incorrectly choose answers C or D. Choice D could describe an effect of *Plessy v. Ferguson*, but not the official thing being sanctioned. Choice A describes the sanction AND the effect of *Plessy v. Ferguson*.

46. D: Civil rights activists used the different "class," or "other white," concept as their legal strategy for the next several decades, and the 14th Amendment was now applied to Hispanics as well as to African Americans. This was the main effect of the *Hernandez v. Texas* decision. It did not have the effect described in choice C, as that happened in a 1970s Supreme Court case. Choice A was the problem being addressed in the Hernandez case, not an effect. And choice B has to do with African Americans, not Hispanics.

47. C: In 1969, *Tinker v. Des Moines* gave students the right to maintain their First Amendment right of free speech; in that case, wearing an armband to protest the Vietnam War, even inside of school buildings (as long as classes were not disrupted). The other cases also involve school districts and education, but were for different specific issues than this one. Although the Bethel and Kuhlmeier cases also touched on the First Amendment, in those cases it was in relation to school assemblies and school newspapers, not school attire.

48. C: President Roosevelt's plan for the judicial branch in 1937 was to raise the total number of Supreme Court justices from 9 to 15. His plan was defeated by the U.S. Senate. The other answer choices sound like plausible ways that one might try to "pack the courts," but they are not correct answers for that time period, which students with a general history knowledge at this grade level should know.

49. D: Writing a letter to your congressperson about an issue that is important to you is the BEST example of how to "lobby" a congressperson. (Visiting, calling, or emailing are other lobbying methods.) Just reading the congressperson's email might be a first step, but not the best example of lobbying. Voting for the congressperson is also just a first step to get him or her into office, and not part of the actual lobbying campaign.

50. D: Student sit-ins were an example in the 1960s of non-violent protesting that took place mostly under the guidance and philosophy of Martin Luther King, Jr. These were not displays of Black Power to incite fear, although those also occurred separately in the 1960s under leaders such as Malcolm X. Sit-ins were not a form of lobbying or litigation, although those are also non-violent in their nature.

How to Overcome Test Anxiety

Just the thought of taking a test is enough to make most people a little nervous. A test is an important event that can have a long-term impact on your future, so it's important to take it seriously and it's natural to feel anxious about performing well. But just because anxiety is normal, that doesn't mean that it's helpful in test taking, or that you should simply accept it as part of your life. Anxiety can have a variety of effects. These effects can be mild, like making you feel slightly nervous, or severe, like blocking your ability to focus or remember even a simple detail.

If you experience test anxiety—whether severe or mild—it's important to know how to beat it. To discover this, first you need to understand what causes test anxiety.

Causes of Test Anxiety

While we often think of anxiety as an uncontrollable emotional state, it can actually be caused by simple, practical things. One of the most common causes of test anxiety is that a person does not feel adequately prepared for their test. This feeling can be the result of many different issues such as poor study habits or lack of organization, but the most common culprit is time management. Starting to study too late, failing to organize your study time to cover all of the material, or being distracted while you study will mean that you're not well prepared for the test. This may lead to cramming the night before, which will cause you to be physically and mentally exhausted for the test. Poor time management also contributes to feelings of stress, fear, and hopelessness as you realize you are not well prepared but don't know what to do about it.

Other times, test anxiety is not related to your preparation for the test but comes from unresolved fear. This may be a past failure on a test, or poor performance on tests in general. It may come from comparing yourself to others who seem to be performing better or from the stress of living up to expectations. Anxiety may be driven by fears of the future—how failure on this test would affect your educational and career goals. These fears are often completely irrational, but they can still negatively impact your test performance.

Elements of Test Anxiety

As mentioned earlier, test anxiety is considered to be an emotional state, but it has physical and mental components as well. Sometimes you may not even realize that you are suffering from test anxiety until you notice the physical symptoms. These can include trembling hands, rapid heartbeat, sweating, nausea, and tense muscles. Extreme anxiety may lead to fainting or vomiting. Obviously, any of these symptoms can have a negative impact on testing. It is important to recognize them as soon as they begin to occur so that you can address the problem before it damages your performance.

The mental components of test anxiety include trouble focusing and inability to remember learned information. During a test, your mind is on high alert, which can help you recall information and stay focused for an extended period of time. However, anxiety interferes with your mind's natural processes, causing you to blank out, even on the questions you know well. The strain of testing during anxiety makes it difficult to stay focused, especially on a test that may take several hours. Extreme anxiety can take a huge mental toll, making it difficult not only to recall test information but even to understand the test questions or pull your thoughts together.

Effects of Test Anxiety

Test anxiety is like a disease—if left untreated, it will get progressively worse. Anxiety leads to poor performance, and this reinforces the feelings of fear and failure, which in turn lead to poor performances on subsequent tests. It can grow from a mild nervousness to a crippling condition. If allowed to progress, test anxiety can have a big impact on your schooling, and consequently on your future.

Test anxiety can spread to other parts of your life. Anxiety on tests can become anxiety in any stressful situation, and blanking on a test can turn into panicking in a job situation. But fortunately, you don't have to let anxiety rule your testing and determine your grades. There are a number of relatively simple steps you can take to move past anxiety and function normally on a test and in the rest of life.

Physical Steps for Beating Test Anxiety

While test anxiety is a serious problem, the good news is that it can be overcome. It doesn't have to control your ability to think and remember information. While it may take time, you can begin taking steps today to beat anxiety.

Just as your first hint that you may be struggling with anxiety comes from the physical symptoms, the first step to treating it is also physical. Rest is crucial for having a clear, strong mind. If you are tired, it is much easier to give in to anxiety. But if you establish good sleep habits, your body and mind will be ready to perform optimally, without the strain of exhaustion. Additionally, sleeping well helps you to retain information better, so you're more likely to recall the answers when you see the test questions.

Getting good sleep means more than going to bed on time. It's important to allow your brain time to relax. Take study breaks from time to time so it doesn't get overworked, and don't study right before bed. Take time to rest your mind before trying to rest your body, or you may find it difficult to fall asleep.

Along with sleep, other aspects of physical health are important in preparing for a test. Good nutrition is vital for good brain function. Sugary foods and drinks may give a burst of energy but this burst is followed by a crash, both physically and emotionally. Instead, fuel your body with protein and vitamin-rich foods.

Also, drink plenty of water. Dehydration can lead to headaches and exhaustion, especially if your brain is already under stress from the rigors of the test. Particularly if your test is a long one, drink water during the breaks. And if possible, take an energy-boosting snack to eat between sections.

Along with sleep and diet, a third important part of physical health is exercise. Maintaining a steady workout schedule is helpful, but even taking 5-minute study breaks to walk can help get your blood pumping faster and clear your head. Exercise also releases endorphins, which contribute to a positive feeling and can help combat test anxiety.

When you nurture your physical health, you are also contributing to your mental health. If your body is healthy, your mind is much more likely to be healthy as well. So take time to rest, nourish your body with healthy food and water, and get moving as much as possible. Taking these physical steps will make you stronger and more able to take the mental steps necessary to overcome test anxiety.

Mental Steps for Beating Test Anxiety

Working on the mental side of test anxiety can be more challenging, but as with the physical side, there are clear steps you can take to overcome it. As mentioned earlier, test anxiety often stems from lack of preparation, so the obvious solution is to prepare for the test. Effective studying may be the most important weapon you have for beating test anxiety, but you can and should employ several other mental tools to combat fear.

First, boost your confidence by reminding yourself of past success—tests or projects that you aced. If you're putting as much effort into preparing for this test as you did for those, there's no reason you should expect to fail here. Work hard to prepare; then trust your preparation.

Second, surround yourself with encouraging people. It can be helpful to find a study group, but be sure that the people you're around will encourage a positive attitude. If you spend time with others who are anxious or cynical, this will only contribute to your own anxiety. Look for others who are motivated to study hard from a desire to succeed, not from a fear of failure.

Third, reward yourself. A test is physically and mentally tiring, even without anxiety, and it can be helpful to have something to look forward to. Plan an activity following the test, regardless of the outcome, such as going to a movie or getting ice cream.

When you are taking the test, if you find yourself beginning to feel anxious, remind yourself that you know the material. Visualize successfully completing the test. Then take a few deep, relaxing breaths and return to it. Work through the questions carefully but with confidence, knowing that you are capable of succeeding.

Developing a healthy mental approach to test taking will also aid in other areas of life. Test anxiety affects more than just the actual test—it can be damaging to your mental health and even contribute to depression. It's important to beat test anxiety before it becomes a problem for more than testing.

Study Strategy

Being prepared for the test is necessary to combat anxiety, but what does being prepared look like? You may study for hours on end and still not feel prepared. What you need is a strategy for test prep. The next few pages outline our recommended steps to help you plan out and conquer the challenge of preparation.

Step 1: Scope Out the Test

Learn everything you can about the format (multiple choice, essay, etc.) and what will be on the test. Gather any study materials, course outlines, or sample exams that may be available. Not only will this help you to prepare, but knowing what to expect can help to alleviate test anxiety.

Step 2: Map Out the Material

Look through the textbook or study guide and make note of how many chapters or sections it has. Then divide these over the time you have. For example, if a book has 15 chapters and you have five days to study, you need to cover three chapters each day. Even better, if you have the time, leave an extra day at the end for overall review after you have gone through the material in depth.

If time is limited, you may need to prioritize the material. Look through it and make note of which sections you think you already have a good grasp on, and which need review. While you are studying, skim quickly through the familiar sections and take more time on the challenging parts.

Write out your plan so you don't get lost as you go. Having a written plan also helps you feel more in control of the study, so anxiety is less likely to arise from feeling overwhelmed at the amount to cover.

Step 3: Gather Your Tools

Decide what study method works best for you. Do you prefer to highlight in the book as you study and then go back over the highlighted portions? Or do you type out notes of the important information? Or is it helpful to make flashcards that you can carry with you? Assemble the pens, index cards, highlighters, post-it notes, and any other materials you may need so you won't be distracted by getting up to find things while you study.

If you're having a hard time retaining the information or organizing your notes, experiment with different methods. For example, try color-coding by subject with colored pens, highlighters, or post-it notes. If you learn better by hearing, try recording yourself reading your notes so you can listen while in the car, working out, or simply sitting at your desk. Ask a friend to quiz you from your flashcards, or try teaching someone the material to solidify it in your mind.

Step 4: Create Your Environment

It's important to avoid distractions while you study. This includes both the obvious distractions like visitors and the subtle distractions like an uncomfortable chair (or a too-comfortable couch that makes you want to fall asleep). Set up the best study environment possible: good lighting and a comfortable work area. If background music helps you focus, you may want to turn it on, but otherwise keep the room quiet. If you are using a computer to take notes, be sure you don't have any other windows open, especially applications like social media, games, or anything else that could distract you. Silence your phone and turn off notifications. Be sure to keep water close by so you stay hydrated while you study (but avoid unhealthy drinks and snacks).

Also, take into account the best time of day to study. Are you freshest first thing in the morning? Try to set aside some time then to work through the material. Is your mind clearer in the afternoon or evening? Schedule your study session then. Another method is to study at the same time of day that you will take the test, so that your brain gets used to working on the material at that time and will be ready to focus at test time.

Step 5: Study!

Once you have done all the study preparation, it's time to settle into the actual studying. Sit down, take a few moments to settle your mind so you can focus, and begin to follow your study plan. Don't give in to distractions or let yourself procrastinate. This is your time to prepare so you'll be ready to fearlessly approach the test. Make the most of the time and stay focused.

Of course, you don't want to burn out. If you study too long you may find that you're not retaining the information very well. Take regular study breaks. For example, taking five minutes out of every hour to walk briskly, breathing deeply and swinging your arms, can help your mind stay fresh.

As you get to the end of each chapter or section, it's a good idea to do a quick review. Remind yourself of what you learned and work on any difficult parts. When you feel that you've mastered the material, move on to the next part. At the end of your study session, briefly skim through your notes again.

But while review is helpful, cramming last minute is NOT. If at all possible, work ahead so that you won't need to fit all your study into the last day. Cramming overloads your brain with more information than it can process and retain, and your tired mind may struggle to recall even previously learned information when it is overwhelmed with last-minute study. Also, the urgent nature of cramming and the stress placed on your brain contribute to anxiety. You'll be more likely to go to the test feeling unprepared and having trouble thinking clearly.

So don't cram, and don't stay up late before the test, even just to review your notes at a leisurely pace. Your brain needs rest more than it needs to go over the information again. In fact, plan to finish your studies by noon or early afternoon the day before the test. Give your brain the rest of the day to relax or focus on other things, and get a good night's sleep. Then you will be fresh for the test and better able to recall what you've studied.

Step 6: Take a Practice Test

Many courses offer sample tests, either online or in the study materials. This is an excellent resource to check whether you have mastered the material, as well as to prepare for the test format and environment.

Check the test format ahead of time: the number of questions, the type (multiple choice, free response, etc.), and the time limit. Then create a plan for working through them. For example, if you have 30 minutes to take a 60-question test, your limit is 30 seconds per question. Spend less time on the questions you know well so that you can take more time on the difficult ones.

If you have time to take several practice tests, take the first one open book, with no time limit. Work through the questions at your own pace and make sure you fully understand them. Gradually work up to taking a test under test conditions: sit at a desk with all study materials put away and set a timer. Pace yourself to make sure you finish the test with time to spare and go back to check your answers if you have time.

After each test, check your answers. On the questions you missed, be sure you understand why you missed them. Did you misread the question (tests can use tricky wording)? Did you forget the information? Or was it something you hadn't learned? Go back and study any shaky areas that the practice tests reveal.

Taking these tests not only helps with your grade, but also aids in combating test anxiety. If you're already used to the test conditions, you're less likely to worry about it, and working through tests until you're scoring well gives you a confidence boost. Go through the practice tests until you feel comfortable, and then you can go into the test knowing that you're ready for it.

Test Tips

On test day, you should be confident, knowing that you've prepared well and are ready to answer the questions. But aside from preparation, there are several test day strategies you can employ to maximize your performance.

First, as stated before, get a good night's sleep the night before the test (and for several nights before that, if possible). Go into the test with a fresh, alert mind rather than staying up late to study.

Try not to change too much about your normal routine on the day of the test. It's important to eat a nutritious breakfast, but if you normally don't eat breakfast at all, consider eating just a protein bar. If you're a coffee drinker, go ahead and have your normal coffee. Just make sure you time it so that the caffeine doesn't wear off right in the middle of your test. Avoid sugary beverages, and drink enough water to stay hydrated but not so much that you need a restroom break 10 minutes into the test. If your test isn't first thing in the morning, consider going for a walk or doing a light workout before the test to get your blood flowing.

Allow yourself enough time to get ready, and leave for the test with plenty of time to spare so you won't have the anxiety of scrambling to arrive in time. Another reason to be early is to select a good seat. It's helpful to sit away from doors and windows, which can be distracting. Find a good seat, get out your supplies, and settle your mind before the test begins.

When the test begins, start by going over the instructions carefully, even if you already know what to expect. Make sure you avoid any careless mistakes by following the directions.

Then begin working through the questions, pacing yourself as you've practiced. If you're not sure on an answer, don't spend too much time on it, and don't let it shake your confidence. Either skip it and come back later, or eliminate as many wrong answers as possible and guess among the remaining ones. Don't dwell on these questions as you continue—put them out of your mind and focus on what lies ahead.

Be sure to read all of the answer choices, even if you're sure the first one is the right answer. Sometimes you'll find a better one if you keep reading. But don't second-guess yourself if you do immediately know the answer. Your gut instinct is usually right. Don't let test anxiety rob you of the information you know.

If you have time at the end of the test (and if the test format allows), go back and review your answers. Be cautious about changing any, since your first instinct tends to be correct, but make sure you didn't misread any of the questions or accidentally mark the wrong answer choice. Look over any you skipped and make an educated guess.

At the end, leave the test feeling confident. You've done your best, so don't waste time worrying about your performance or wishing you could change anything. Instead, celebrate the successful completion of this test. And finally, use this test to learn how to deal with anxiety even better next time.

Review Video: Test Anxiety
Visit mometrix.com/academy and enter code: 100340

Important Qualification

Not all anxiety is created equal. If your test anxiety is causing major issues in your life beyond the classroom or testing center, or if you are experiencing troubling physical symptoms related to your anxiety, it may be a sign of a serious physiological or psychological condition. If this sounds like your situation, we strongly encourage you to seek professional help.

Online Resources

Due to our efforts to try to keep this book to a manageable length, we've created a link that will give you access to all of your online resources:

mometrix.com/resources719/ssregushistgov

It's Your Moment, Let's Celebrate It!

Share your story @mometrixtestpreparation